CLEAR VISION
accountancy · consultancy

January 2011

Clear Vision Accountancy Group Limited
1 Abacus House
Newlands Road
Corsham
Wiltshire
SN13 0BH

Telephone: 01249 712074
Fax: 01249 716242
Web: www.clearvisiondental.co.uk
www.clearvisionaccountancygroup.co.uk

The Business of Dentistry

How You Run a Successful and Profitable Dental Practice

00 Contents

Foreword

Today, in nearly every developed country, private dental practices are highly complex and fiercely competitive enterprises. Complex, given dentists must understand and successfully fulfill many accountabilities, both in the clinical domain as well as the business domain. Fiercely competitive, given the fact their markets are quite narrow for patients who can afford more advanced dental procedures.

First and foremost, the dentist in private practice must become a state -of-the -art clinician. Advances in clinical and digital technology, disease management and cosmetic dentistry are occurring at an extremely high velocity. Materials, methods and techniques continue to dramatically progress. With the advances in computerization, 3-D imaging, implants, bone regenerative techniques, along with a host of other cutting-edge materials and treatments, correlated with the tremendous increase in knowledge of dental disease, esthetics, and wound healing, dentists are hard pressed to stay on the leading edge. To stay competitive, dentists must learn to continuously embody these advances. This alone requires a great deal of time, financial investment, education and training, far beyond their time in their practice.

As important for dentists in private practice, the delivery of their dentistry occurs within a business context. To succeed in business requires many critical nonclinical functions to be performed and a wide variety of activities to be accomplished. These functions and activities fall into four basic domains, leadership, management, ownership and marketing. So besides being a top-class clinician, dentists also need to become top-flight businessmen and businesswomen.

One domain to be mastered in this business context is leadership. Leadership is the ability to envision a future, a future that's possible and has others inspired and committed to achieving that future. A future based on core values. A future which makes a difference for patients and is fulfilling for staff. A future that incites loyalty and affinity from staff and patients.

A future that has a clear and powerful purpose. A future that gives rise to a compelling mission. Any dental practice that lacks leadership is doomed to struggle or fail.

Then there is management, the ability to produce actions and results through others. In a dental practice there are a multitude of activities which require members of staff to be fully responsible for fulfilling. Functions from administrative to clinical, from customer relations to operating sophisticated diagnostic equipment, from delivering dental care to managing financial transactions. There are hundreds of activities and outcomes that require management in a for-profit dental practice.

The majority of revenues are generated while the dentist is at chair-side. Unlike many other businesses, the time allotted for management and leadership is severely constrained. So the dentist must be able to effectively manage and powerfully lead his or her staff in the brief amount of time available.

Another domain that must be fully mastered is ownership. Ownership brings a particular level of demand and rigor to the enterprise. Owners seek a return on their investment. Owners hold leadership and management accountable to produce the necessary results so that the enterprise is profitable. Owners watch cash flow and expenses closely. Owners operate consistently within a budget. Owners think and act not only for the present, but for the long term. Owners understand that without being profitable, you can't have a successful business.

And finally there is marketing, the ability to communicate a dentist's distinct brand to the market so that he or she attracts and retains patients. The dentist must communicate through various channels and media the benefits that his or her practice provides to potential patients that makes the practice special. The dentist must incite current patients to powerfully communicate a practice's value to their friends, family and coworkers, motivating them to become patients. Marketing makes the market aware of your services in such a way they seek your services.

To be successful, a dentist must master these four domains of business. Rob Walsh's "Business of Dentistry" does a brilliant job of educating dentists on how to be successful in each of these four domains. This book goes into great depth in each of these areas as well as presenting particularly well done charts and checklists for dentists to evaluate their status in each of these four domains of business.

I've been in the dental industry for more than 37 years as a private practitioner, academician, researcher, author and 25 years as a practice management and organizational consultant. I've read many books on practice management, but none as in-depth, as well written, and as complete as Rob Walsh's Business of Dentistry. If you want to master running your practice as a successful business, I strongly recommend reading this book.

Dr. Marc B. Cooper
CEO and President
The Mastery Company
www.masterycompany.com

Author profile

Rob began his career as a chartered accountant. He worked his way up the ladder over a period of eight years to become partner in a six-partner firm.

Rob recognised that as an accountant he was in an ideal position to not only help business owners measure their numbers, but also to help them change them and achieve their personal goals. But this was something he felt he could not do effectively in his present role. So in 2003 he formed the Clear Vision Accountancy Group ("CVAG") to pursue this vision.

Through CVAG, Rob has found his vocation; helping to make a difference to the lives of business owners. He works with them closely, helping them define their goals every year and also assisting them in reaching them.

He has helped hundreds of business owners to get more of what they want from their lives. His notable track record includes an innovative action plan which successfully increased the turnover of a manufacturing business from £1.6m to £4m within the space of three years.

It was after he started working with a dentist in 2001 that Rob realised the potential to help business owners in the dental sector. As he explains: *"It is clear that many dentists struggle to find the time to step away from their businesses. They are tied to them on a daily basis. As a result their quality of life suffers. Their families suffer. And they rarely get the rewards they deserve."*

This was the driving factor in creating Clear Vision Dental Consultancy ("CVDC"), a thriving consultancy firm which is helping around 50 dentists at any one time – see www.clearvisiondental.co.uk.

Rob is a man who most definitely 'walks his talk'. CVAG is in the top 5% profitable accountancy firms and CVDC continues to gain plaudits.

But these results are not achieved at the expense of Rob's own life – he enjoys 13 weeks holiday a year and spend an additional six weeks working on the strategy for his business.

Rob hopes you will enjoy and benefit from this book. A great first step to take once you have read the book is to log on to the Clear Vision Dental website: www.clearvisiondental.co.uk, and complete the checklist which measures your business on the 5 key factors proven to give dentists greater results and bigger rewards. Complete this and you will discover where your practice is strong and the areas where it can improve. Plus you will ABSOLUTELY, DEFINITELY know where to start to improve your results and increase the rewards you see from your practice.

Acknowledgements

I wish to acknowledge the people who have contributed and supported me in creating this book.

Thank you to Sue, my lovely wife and my lovely children Amy and Chloe who continue to support me in achieving my goals.

To my parents Roy and Felicity, brother Neil and godparents Jillian and Dennis Slade, you have all been there for me at all times whether they have been highs or lows.

The Clear Vision team who have contributed towards the success of the business and continue to allow me to fulfil my vision. The journey together is enjoyable.

To the Executive Board, Tony Swift and Paul Shrimpling who have been and continue to be great friends and who give direction when it is needed.

The dental professionals committed to helping dentists to be all they can be – Medenta, Essential Money, Gaynor Barrett and Cohen Cramer to name but a few.

To the book team, Jeff Senior and Dee Gerrish (Clear Vision Group Marketing Manager) who have assisted in the creation of the book. Also Dr Andrea Ubhi and Marc Cooper for their input and feedback.

I would like to thank Steve Pipe and his team at AVN for their support, inspiration and insights over the last ten years. And also to thank AVN and all the other business gurus who allowed me to refer to and build on some of their innovative tools and ideas within these pages. I hope to make as much of a difference to the dental profession as they have done to the accounting profession.

This book is dedicated to the dentists, Clear Vision clients,
who have allowed me to share their professional and personal lives,
and in memory of Chris Walsh - a great bloke.

You have directly contributed to the success of my business
and my growth as a human being.

This book is thanks to you all.

Leadership

I urge you to read this section of the book.

It's so important you read it because it gives you the foundations to make your dental practice a success.

Read this section, learn the lessons and apply the insights. You'll then ensure your practice has a solid platform for growth.

Once you've established your platform for growth, you can move on to other sections in the book that will fill in the details and ensure your overall strategy is a success.

01 The Role of a Leader

We are in a world of increasing change – technological change, regulatory change, changes in customer expectations.

So our businesses need to continually change.

Only leadership can overcome the sources of corporate inertia and bring about the actions needed to alter behaviour in any significant way. So to rise to the challenges of the 21st century you need to develop strong leadership.

In his book *Leading Change*, John P. Kotter predicts that – since leadership deals mostly with change and the rate of change is increasing all the time – the organisation of the future will have to become much more skilled at creating leaders; people who can create and communicate a vision and strategies. And this will only happen through a programme of lifelong learning.

This is backed up by the findings of Jim Collins and Jerry I. Porras. For their book *Built to Last*, they spent six years studying exceptional companies – visionary companies – to see what accounts for their success. In the 18 visionary companies, they found that only 4 times, in a combined 1,700 years, did one of the visionary companies go outside the firm to appoint a leader! They all had processes in place to develop people as leaders from within their organisations.

The purpose of this chapter is to get you to think about the role of a leader. It will allow you to assess your own leadership skills and help you to identify those areas you may need to improve to become an even better leader.

Because without good leadership skills within your business, the 'building the perfect 21st-century practice' change process will *fail*.

> What is leadership?

Leadership defines what the future should look like, aligns people with that vision and inspires them to make it happen despite the obstacles.

Sir John Harvey-Jones said that 'Leaders should only do what only they can do.' But what exactly is that? What should you be doing as a leader?

The rest of this chapter focuses on the core tasks that you should be doing as a leader.

> The core tasks that belong to a leader

These are the things that you **MUST** do as a leader.

1. Define your values and live by them.
2. Establish direction.
3. Decide on strategy.
4. Build an unstoppable team.
5. Set up systems to feedback key information.
6. Drive the business forward.

Each of these tasks will now be explored in further detail.

> Define your values and live by them

As a leader, you must be the person that creates the right culture within your business.

Jim Collins and Jerry I. Porras found that one of the fundamental elements in the visionary companies they studied was what they called a core ideology; the core values and sense of purpose that guides and inspires people throughout the organisation.

The core values are the organisation's essential and enduring tenets – a small set of guiding principles.

The core purpose is the organisation's fundamental reasons for existence beyond just making money. It is not to be confused with specific goals or business strategies, which change over time. Core purpose should not change, although it should inspire change. For example, the core purpose of Walt Disney is 'to make people happy'.

The core purpose has a key role in guiding and inspiring. It goes beyond just making money because this does not inspire people at all levels of the organisation and it does not provide much guidance.

So what is your core ideology?

There is no right or wrong core ideology; it is what you believe in. In the visionary companies, Jim Collins and Jerry I. Porras found that no single item showed up consistently. For some companies their customers were central to their ideology. To others it was their team, to others their products or services. Or risk taking. Or innovation.

They found that it was the authenticity of the ideology and the extent to which a company attains consistent alignment with the ideology that counted more than the content. And they found that the very act of stating a core ideology influences behaviour towards consistency with that ideology.

As a result of stating their core ideology, the visionary companies more thoroughly indoctrinated their team into it, more carefully nurtured and selected senior management based on their fit with it and more consistently aligned their goals, strategies, tactics and organisational design.

By influencing behaviour, stating a core ideology will impact on the culture within your business. And since many challenges within most of the practices we come across stem from a bad culture, then working on your core ideology is a great starting point in developing the right culture for your business.

However, if your core ideology is not passionately held on a gut level then it is not core. It needs to be meaningful and inspirational to you and your team.

> Establish direction

Your role is also to establish the direction your business is going in, to develop a clear vision of the future and to develop strategies. And then produce the changes needed to achieve that vision. John P. Kotter defines vision as 'a picture of the future with some implicit or explicit commentary on why people should strive to create that future'.

Developing your vision is a creative process; think of it as translating the vision from words into pictures, of creating an image that people can carry around in their heads. You may know that the international business guru Michael Gerber tells us that one of the most powerful things you can do is have a designer come in and paint a picture of what your business will look like when it is finally done.

Your description of what your business will look like must have passion, emotion and conviction. It must be something that you personally believe in. It must be truly exciting to those inside the business. And it must be so clear and compelling that it does not require any explanation.

In their book *Built to Last*, Collins and Porras found that all the visionary companies had a clear and compelling vision for the future. In fact, they referred to this vision as a BHAG (Big Hairy Audacious Goal).

To be a fully fledged BHAG the vision should fall outside your comfort zone, it should take you to a truly exciting place where it will continue to stimulate progress (even after the leaders disappear) and it should be consistent with your *core ideology*.

The characteristics of an effective vision are:

- **Imaginable** – it should paint a clear picture in people's minds.
- **Desirable** – it should appeal to all the stakeholders in a business and should convey passion, emotion and conviction.
- **Audacious** – is ambitious enough to force people out of their comfort zones and take them to a truly exciting place...
- **Feasible** – ... but at the same time it should be attainable.
- **Focused** – is clear enough to provide guidance in decision-making.
- **Flexible** – is general enough to allow individual initiative and alternative responses in light of changing conditions.
- **Communicable** – is articulated with clarity so that it requires little explanation and can be understood within five minutes.

So, as a leader you need to create your vision for the future. This is the starting point for everything. As Michael Gerber says, 'What does it look like when it's finally done?' And Dr Stephen Covey tells us to 'start with the end in mind'.

However, your vision cannot be created in a single meeting. It may take several months, or even years, to create a great vision. Both analytical thinking and a lot of dreaming are essential throughout the activity.

A great vision serves three important purposes, it:

1. clarifies the general direction for your business
2. motivates people to take action in the right direction
3. helps coordinate the actions of different people by aligning them.

So once you have created your vision for the future you must communicate that vision to the team. If you cannot describe your vision to someone in five minutes and get his or her interest, you have more work to do. By communicating direction in both words and deeds, you will align people. This is an important early step to building an unstoppable team.

> Decide on strategy

Strategy provides both logic and a first level of detail to show how a vision can be accomplished.

Although there are many definitions of strategy, a simple but effective definition is: 'Considering the alternative ways of getting to point B'. Point B is where you want to be in the future – your vision. And, inevitably, there will be more than one way of getting there. You need to consider all of those routes and then choose the best one.

John P. Kotter provides us with a useful illustration of where strategy fits with vision, the role of a leader and management.

The relationship of vision, strategies, plans and budgets

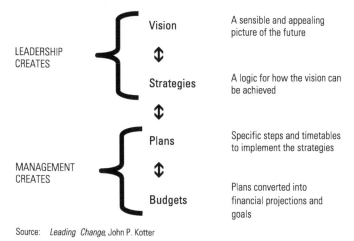

LEADERSHIP CREATES	Vision	A sensible and appealing picture of the future
	Strategies	A logic for how the vision can be achieved
MANAGEMENT CREATES	Plans	Specific steps and timetables to implement the strategies
	Budgets	Plans converted into financial projections and goals

Source: *Leading Change,* John P. Kotter

Once vision, values and strategy have been defined, the rest of you business plan will flow from that.

> Build an unstoppable team

A key role of a leader is to get the very best out of people. In fact, in their book The Firm of the Future, Paul Dunn and Ron Baker believe that, 'Attracting, retaining and rewarding human capital is the single most important role of leadership.' Even if you do not agree that it is the single most important role, it is undoubtedly one of the most important roles of leadership.

Here are some key areas you need to work on to build an unstoppable team.

- **Getting the right people** – at the end of the day, recruitment is a marketing issue. And since this is probably the number one issue for many businesses, it must be done extraordinarily well.

- **Goals and vision** – you must inspire people with your vision for the organisation. Having a clear vision and communicating that to the team is an important first step. And then make sure that everything that you do is congruent with that vision and with the core values. Make sure that you walk the talk.

- **Communication** – communication is more than just communicating goals and vision. Communication should be two-way. Great leaders listen as well as talk. You must be ready to listen to your team, and to act on what you hear. It is also important to let people know when complaints have been dealt with, or ideas implemented, or else people will feel they have been talking to a brick wall.

- **Development, promotion and learning** – you should continually train and develop your team. Training should include soft skills (e.g. time management and delegation) as well as the technical skills for doing the job. Development includes listening to your team. Find out what they want from life and help them develop their career path to achieve what they want.

- **Culture** – getting the right culture is not easy, but it is vitally important. Create a culture of mutual respect, mutual trust and mutual support. And make the workplace a fun place to be.

- **Recognition, appreciation and rewards** – money is important, but it is not necessarily the most important thing. Recognition and appreciation go a long way to getting the best out of your team.

- **Leadership and management style** – you need to be honest about your style of leadership and management. If you are not getting the best out of your team, it is a sign that you need to change.

It is well worth reading The Richer Way for the dozens of ideas for creating fun, recognising people, rewarding people, developing communication mechanisms and generating loyalty.

> Set up systems to feedback key information

As a leader, you will need to make key decisions on a regular basis.

The quality of those decisions will depend upon the quality of the information you have available. Only with good and wide-ranging information can you develop a view of where your business is and whether it is moving in the right direction. So essential information needs to be fed back to you on a regular basis.

A key tool is the One Page™ Plan – which you will find in Chapter 16, page 60. In essence, the One Page™ Plan is exactly what its name suggests – a business plan that fits on a single sheet of A4.

The plan starts at the bottom of the page and works upwards. So it starts with your vision. That vision, in turn, determines the key areas in which the business will have to excel in order to achieve its goals (i.e. the *underlying success drivers*). Next come the key factors that directly drive the business's sales, costs and cash flow. And finally there are the key results that have been generated by all the underlying drivers (these key results are deliberately positioned at the top of the page because they are the *consequence* of everything below them on the page).

In this way the plan describes all the key factors behind the business's success, and maps them out in a logical way that mirrors the causal links between goals, success drivers and eventual results.

Not only does this give you an early warning system (by systematically measuring and monitoring everything that is really important in the business)…

… but it also acts as a catalyst for identifying the action that needs to be taken, and for recording and monitoring the constantly updated action plans that the business plan contains.

It is simple and readily understandable by everybody within the team. It should be shared with the team so that *everybody* knows exactly what the business is trying to achieve, how far it has got towards achieving it and what they can do to get the business there even faster.

So you should create your version of the One Page™ Plan and the systems to feed back the information required.

> Drive the business forward

The world is constantly changing. And the rate of change is increasing.

So standing still is not an option. You need to change almost everything: culture, strategy, tactics, operations, policies, goals and so on. The only thing that should not change over time is your core ideology (your guiding principles and fundamental reason for being).

As a leader you must drive the business forward. You need the ability to question and challenge accepted practices and a restless desire to find a better way. Great leaders are never satisfied; they always want to see things improve. The mark of great leadership is to have this search for improvement permeating the entire organisation.

You must drive the change; without one person tirelessly demanding improvements, it will lose momentum. You must act as a coach for the team.

There are five basic lessons we can learn from visionary companies.

1. Give it a try – and quick! No matter what, don't sit still. Try a lot of stuff and keep what works. Tom Peters used the acronym 'SAV' – which stands for 'screwing around vigorously'.
2. Accept that mistakes will be made – and build a 'no blame' culture.
3. Take small steps – because lots of small steps can lead to significant strategic shifts.
4. Give people the room they need – allow your team to persist with ideas.
5. Build tangible mechanisms (i.e. systems and processes) that promote innovation. For example, the 15 per cent rule at 3M allows technical people to spend up to 15 per cent of their time on their own projects.

In fact, visionary companies realise that staying in comfort zones is not the objective. So they install powerful systems to create discomfort – to obliterate complacency – and thereby stimulate change and improvement before the external world demands it. These systems and tangible mechanisms include:

- Internal competition.

- A strategy of consciously yielding market share as products become low-margin commodities, thus forcing it to produce new innovations in order to grow and prosper.

- At General Electric groups of team members meet to discuss opportunities for improvement – upper managers are not allowed to participate in the discussion but must make on-the-spot decisions about the proposals in front of the whole group.

- Boeing assigns managers the task of developing strategy as if they worked for a competing company with the aim of obliterating Boeing.

- Sam Walton began using a mechanism called 'Beat Yesterday' ledger books. These ledger books tracked sales figures on a daily basis in comparison to the exact same day of the week one year earlier.

- A great mechanism for a practice is the concept of focus groups.

> Take an honest look at yourself

As a leader you must take personal responsibility for everything that is not right about your business.

Does your team feel inspired? Do they feel part of a team that knows where it is going? Do they buy into your vision for the business and understand the strategy for achieving that vision? Do they find you are a good decision-maker? Do people feel they are given enough information or do they think you keep them in the dark? Do they have confidence that you will do what you say you will do? Do your managers believe that you delegate enough to them and allow them to get on with their job?

Answer these questions honestly.

If something is not right in your business then it is a sign that there is something that you've got to learn; something that you've got to change. And that may need to start with a change within you. You may recall that Michael Gerber tells us that our business is a mirror of us. If our business is disorganised it is because we are disorganised. If our people are angry it is because we are making them angry.

Until leaders admit that they make mistakes, they cannot be truly effective. One of the most important steps on the way to being a great leader is to ensure that you learn every day. The key is to admit to yourself that however many years you've been in business, you don't know everything and you can always learn and improve.

So what steps will you take to become a better leader?

> *Suggested further reading*

Start to build a library of books and audiobooks on leadership, vision, strategy and people/personal development. You need to continually develop your own leadership skills and the leadership skills of your team.

Here are some suggestions as a starting point for that library.

Built to Last, Jim Collins and Jerry I. Porras

Good to Great, Jim Collins

Gung Ho!, Ken Blanchard and Sheldon Bowles

How to Transform Your Company and Enjoy It!, Ken Lewis and Stephen Lytton

Leading Change, John P. Kotter

Principle-Centred Leadership, Stephen R. Covey

Richer on Leadership, Julian Richer

Who Moved My Cheese?, Dr Spencer Johnson

02 The Future Matters

A clear vision makes a significant difference to your dental practice

> A man with no vision is no man at all.
>
> *Unknown*

In business as in life, it's important you have a vision.

No vision = No direction.

With a vision, you have something to work towards.

And a personal vision inspires you to act; it drives you on so you can make it a reality. If you have no clear vision, you have no target to aim for, nothing against which you can measure your performance.

Avoid acting aimlessly; be sure you have a vision.

> The most pathetic person in the world is someone who has sight but no vision.
>
> *Helen Keller*

You must focus on what you want to achieve and how you're going to do it.

Envisage where you'll be in a year, in three years, in ten years. Your vision can be anything you want as long as it is realistic and achievable.

You may see yourself on a yacht in the Caribbean in five years' time, having sold a successful practice and retired to a life in the sun. An achievable and worthwhile reward is a great incentive, a great driver to right-action.

Having a vision isn't necessarily just about money or about building a successful business.

You might want to break the mould. You might want to create a different dental practice, one that stands out from the crowd. You might want to have a practice with an outstanding image and reputation, with a level and type of service way above the norm.

People happily pay for a superior, personalised service – a phone call on the day of the appointment, a reserved parking space, an attentive team and the tiny details to make their visit truly memorable.

Which neatly brings us back to money, because you can charge more if the service justifies it.

Butterfly Dental

Bob Mehay, a dentist in Manchester, has a clear vision of what he wants his practice to look like.

He has created an all-glass double frontage to the property. His patients now go up glass steps, with under-step lighting, and enter through two glass sliding doors.

Then, as they enter the practice, he backs this up with a patient experience worthy of notice too.

Patients are met with a smile and genuine caring attention.

The service his patients receive also has an attention to detail most practices ignore or take for granted.

His vision, in effect, is to create a spectacular practice and provide a level of service to match.

Bob knows that his patients will value his service based on what they see and experience. He knows they don't have the skills to rate his team on their clinical abilities.

He has created an experience his patients rave about and are willing to pay for.

> *Look after the roots*

Think of your business vision as a lily pad on a pond.

To grow and flourish, your vision needs the support of a massive root system, including your core values (Chapter 3), mission (Chapter 6), team members (Chapter 14) and company systems (Chapter 19).

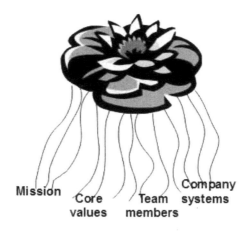

If your vision doesn't have a root system, it dies. So it's vital you create and nurture the root system to allow it to flourish.

Don't get totally sucked into the day-to-day running of the practice so you have no time to look at the overall picture. If you do, the roots will wither away and the lily pad won't flourish.

> Stay focused

> When you start in business, you are the entrepreneur. How long before you become a technician?
>
> **Michael Gerber**

In the beginning, your vision might be to become an entrepreneur, create a successful practice and an income for life.

You incorporate an exit plan with options so, at some specified point in the future, you can choose to sell (or keep going).

The danger is, as the years pass, your clear vision fades into the background and you get bogged down with the day-to-day work of your practice.

It's absolutely vital your vision stays fresh and you remain focused on it. Otherwise, you lose sight of your aims and never achieve what you want.

Your vision is personal and a picture of where you want to be at a point in the future.

You need to communicate your vision to the rest of your team because they're vital in helping you achieve it. Telling your patients isn't necessary; you just need to point them in the right direction.

A crucial aspect of your vision is that it must be flexible. Things never stay the same and, as the world changes, you may need to adapt your vision to reflect these changes.

You may have new health and safety regulations to comply with or changes to your clinical requirements. These may impose additional costs on your practice or offer the possibilities of additional income.

So you need to keep an open mind, have a positive outlook and adapt accordingly. Your vision is a moveable feast rather than something set in stone.

> Vision and action

There is a view…

… if you have no vision, you have no practice at all!

Although a bit extreme, you most definitely have a better, more focused and ultimately more satisfying practice if you have a vision to aim for.

So what next?

> Vision without action is merely a dream. Action without vision just passes the time. Vision with action can change the world.
>
> **Joel A. Barker**

Having decided on your vision, you must take action to make it happen.

How about you start by getting your team focused on your vision too?

It's important you understand your personal and business goals, communicate your aims and have a strategy and systems to make it all happen.

Next, we'll discuss how you *turn your vision into right-action*.

03 First Principles

Why your dental practice needs clear core values

> **Leaders honour their core values but they are flexible in how they execute them.**
>
> *Colin Powell*

Your core values are the essential guiding principles you use to run your business.

Core values set out what a business stands for. They define and represent what your business aims to be. And they must be imprinted right through it.

At Clear Vision, for example, we try to create an enjoyable atmosphere for everyone – we have space hoppers and a jukebox.

We believe everyone is an equal member of the team. Partners and managers work in the same space as other members of the team. There are no separate executive offices.

We also believe in sharing information throughout the team. That means everyone sees financial information and they know the turnover and profit every month.

Your practice will have the core values that are important to you – ethical, friendly, trustworthy, honest, innovative, clear communications – they can be anything you want.

Whatever you choose, core values help in many ways providing you stick with them.

If your core values feature 'excellence', this must be apparent in everything you do, so you:

- answer incoming phone calls promptly and efficiently
- deal with patients' questions quickly and fully
- meet and greet patients in a first-rate manner
- talk to and about patients in a professional and friendly way.

Never gloss over or ignore anything.

What if things don't work out?

It's important you deal with any failure to adhere to core values.

But this should take the form of a discussion and a solution rather than an admonishment.

Be positive rather than negative.

> *All in together*

Core values are central to your practice.

It's vital everyone upholds them fully.

How do you ensure this happens? You make sure everyone knows what the core values are and how they are achieved.

Every member of your team has to 'buy into' these principles. When they do, you can achieve them.

Ideally, your patients should have the same core values as your practice.

If some patients cause problems and clearly don't fit in, it's best to ask them to find another dentist.

This might seem a bold or foolish move. But when all your patients have the same core values it makes it more likely you achieve all your aims.

Core values are important to set the right team spirit. Everyone pulls in the same direction.

04 Set Personal Goals

Why planning the endgame is vital for the success of your dental practice

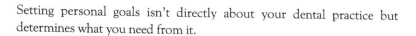

> To become fully alive, a person must have goals and aims that transcend himself.
>
> **Herbert A. Otto**

Setting personal goals isn't directly about your dental practice but determines what you need from it.

What do you want from life?

Your personal goals establish what your practice needs to provide for you to achieve whatever you want. So it's vital you know your personal goals, otherwise you can't properly plan the rest.

To help work out your personal goals, ask yourself a few questions:

Family goals
- What is your current work/life balance like?
- How would you like to improve this?
- What do you want for your children's education?
- Do you feel you need to spend more time with your family?

Free time
- Would you like more free time?
- How much holiday do you currently take?
- How much would you like in the future and by what date?

Retirement
- When would you like to retire?
- How much income do you need in retirement?
- What is your retirement pot currently?

Travel	• Where would you like to travel and in what year?
Health goals	• What are these and by when?
Financial goals	• What is your current mortgage? • When would you like to clear the mortgage? • Do you have any other debts? If so, how much? • What is the cost of any property you want to buy and when do you want to buy it? • What is the value of your investment portfolio? • Would you like to buy a holiday/second home?
Hobbies	• Are there any courses or lifetime learning you would like to do?
Assets	• Have you any ambitions to own a particular car or boat?
Achievements	• Do you want to become a public speaker or run a marathon? • Anything else you want to do?

Establishing your current and preferred work/life balance are is the most important questions issue. Your practice has to provide more than just work and an income; it must give you a happy and contented life.

It's essential you determine how happy you are in yourself and where you can make improvements:

Are you happy with the practice?
Do you have a contented family life?
Do you spend enough time with your family?
Are you healthy?

Is money a problem?
Do you have an enjoyable social life?
Do you contribute to charity?

Setting personal goals also means deciding upon the following:

How many hours do you want to work each week?
How many number of weeks' holiday do you want to take each year?
When do you want to be debt- free?
How much money do you need to live on for the rest of your life?

A goal properly set is halfway reached.

Abraham Lincoln

Setting personal goals is like being at the base of a mountain range when you want to be on top of the sixth mountain. You have to work out how you're going to get there and when.

> Formulate your exit plan

A large part of setting personal goals is creating an exit plan; a plan where you are debt-free and have an income for life that comfortably meets your needs.

An exit plan simply sets a point in time when you are able to decide what you want to do.

- Do I sell the business and retire abroad?

- Shall I keep going for a few more years?

- Can I bring in a partner to share the responsibility and realise some of my investment?

- Will I pass the business in succession to family members?

When setting your personal goals, you're not saying what you will do when the exit point is reached. What you do is aim to put yourself in a position when you can decide what you want to do.

> Planning example

Take the example of a dentist in Manchester who has:

- a £500,000 annual turnover

- relatively low profitability

- two young children and a wife who doesn't work

- a general unhappiness with the business of dentistry

- no clear vision of where he wants his practice to go

- a wish to be debt-free at 60 with £80,000 annual income for the rest of his life.

The aim is to rekindle the dentist's passion for the business and to set an exit plan.

If the practice isn't making enough profit to clear debts by age 60, how is this to be achieved?

Typically, the dentist will have three main assets:

- the family home
- the dental property
- the dental business.

The first step is to organise the assets to generate the required annual income, repay all debts and leave the home mortgage-free by retirement. This may be achieved, for example, by:

- borrowing on the dental property (currently no debt but with tax relief available)
- investing in the home to create extra value
- buying other property (such as buy-to-lets) to generate additional income
- paying off other high-interest debts (such as credit cards).

Banks don't normally lend against the turnover of a practice. However, specifically for the healthcare sector (including care homes, doctors and dentists), they lend against goodwill.

Next, the dentist determines, at retirement, where income can be sourced:

The relationship of vision, strategies, plans and budgets

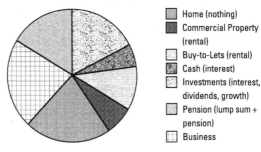

Home (nothing)
Commercial Property (rental)
Buy-to-Lets (rental)
Cash (interest)
Investments (interest, dividends, growth)
Pension (lump sum + pension)
Business

If you need £80,000 gross per annum:

- buy-to-lets (if debt-free) may generate £12,000

- pension (including state pension) may contribute £24,000

- business assets, if worth £400,000, could provide £20,000 at 5% interest.

This leaves a funding gap of £24,000 per annum. In the years leading up to retirement, the dentist needs to find the assets that will generate this additional income. Perhaps:

- increase the value of the practice

- buy other assets

- make additional pension contributions.

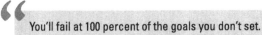

" You'll fail at 100 percent of the goals you don't set.

Mark Victor Hansen

"

Once a financial plan is in place, the dentist can focus on the practice with a positive mindset.

Make this calculation for yourself.

Once you know the size of your funding gap, you can decide what you need to do to fill it.

If you feel you can't manage this yourself, a company such as Essential Money Limited can help with personal financial planning.

The overall aim is to build your dental practice and make your assets work harder.

> Be SMART

All personal goals are individual.

The important point is to make sure they are 'SMART':

- **S**pecific
- **M**emorable
- **A**chievable
- **R**elevant
- **T**imely

You need to assess what each goal is, how you will achieve it and when.

And having set your SMART goals, you must ensure they stay on track.

This may mean you work harder and longer in the early stages, then tail off when everything is running smoothly.

> The Harvard Business School tracked 100 individuals from leaving school. Three of them set personal goals and stuck to them. These three achieved more value than the other ninety-seven together.

Setting personal goals is vital. Don't underestimate the task.

05 Define Your Business Goals

The need for a proper structure

> Think little goals and expect little achievements. Think big goals and win big success.
>
> **David J. Schwarz**

Setting business goals is vital because they determine the role you play in your practice.

Business goals are closely linked to your personal goals. If you don't achieve them, the chances of meeting your personal goals are slim to nil.

Your business goals determine how your practice will look, feel and perform.

In order to establish what these goals are, the questions you need to answer include:

- What is your current practice turnover/income?
- What would you like your turnover to be?
- Would you like to work more or fewer hours?
- Do you like the role you currently have in the practice?
- If not, what would you prefer to be working on?
- Are there any inefficiencies in the practice that need to be addressed?
- Do you require any changes in the practice structure or delegation of work?
- Are there any team or organisation issues?
- Is recruitment required?

- Is it an NHS or private patient practice?

- Do you have goals in terms of location or premises?

- How many sites and surgeries do you have now and want in the future?

- What is the endgame?

  – To sell the practice? If so, for how much and by what date?
  – If it is succession to family members, which ones?
  – To stay in business as long as you can?

- Are there any team training requirements?

- Do you want to change the practice image?

- Is systemisation of the practice required?

- Is the financial function good enough or are management accounts required?

- What type of work do you want the practice to offer? You may want to provide additional services such as whitening or specialise in implants.

- Is specialist training required to provide this work?

- Do you need to recruit specialist team members to handle particular aspects of the work?

Your personal goals may impact on your business goals. If, for example, a personal goal is to reduce your time from five-day to three-day working while a business goal is to specialise in implants, recruitment will be essential.

> *Structure your practice*

An outcome of setting your business goals is you establish a business structure that divides the practice into three separate areas.

In each of these areas there are various services, which are fulfilled by separate roles and have different profit margins associated with them.

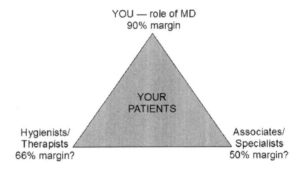

YOU — role of MD
90% margin

YOUR
PATIENTS

Hygienists/
Therapists
66% margin?

Associates/
Specialists
50% margin?

The business structure you create must be flexible. Situations change and demand for dental services alters with them.

For instance, when times are hard, the demand for cosmetic services isn't as high. So you have to be prepared for alterations to the work mix in each area.

People with goals succeed because they know where they're going. It's as simple as that.

Zig Zigler

Each business goal you set needs a strategy to determine how you achieve it.

If you set a goal to expand from one site to three sites, you must have a strategy to enable you to get there. This is covered in Chapter 7.

Before you set your business goals, ask yourself a question: 'If I fail to achieve my goals, will I feel unfulfilled?'

If the answer is 'yes', make sure you don't set yourself up to fail. Don't set goals that are impossible to achieve, keep track of progress and get the strategy right to hit your targets.

As with your personal goals, make sure your business goals are SMART (see page 29).

06 On a Mission

Define why you are in business

Setting out your mission is key because it defines the core purpose of your practice.

Many company mission statements come across as meaningless PR jargon. Consequently, people don't understand them and ignore them.

Don't make the same mistake. Your mission can be anything you want it to be as long as you really believe in it and it is achievable.

You may simply aim to be a traditional dentist – there's nothing wrong with that.

You may want to 'create the smile you desire' for your patients.

As long as you believe in it and abide by it, that's fine. But don't just set it and forget it – stick to it.

How do you decide on your mission?

Appendix A (see page i) defines how to create the perfect mission statement to point you in the right direction. There's a mission statement checklist so you get it right and include everything important.

But remember, your mission statement is personal to you. You need to make it work.

To do that, you must have the help of others and you must embed the mission within the other elements of your practice.

> " If you are a bus driver, your mission is to point the bus in the right direction.
> If the people on the bus are your team, you have to get the wrong people off the bus and ensure the others are in the correct places. The bus conductor (your practice or business manager) will help you achieve your mission.
>
> *from Good to Great by **Jim Collins***
> "

Remember why you're in business in the first place. Be specific and set your mission around your reason for being in the dentistry business.

Be passionate about achieving your mission and vision.

07 Point-to-Point

Set strategies to guide you along the path to success

> Strategy is a style of thinking. A conscious and deliberate process. An intensive implementation system. The science of ensuring future success.
>
> **Pete Johnson**

To achieve your practice vision and mission, you must complete a number of milestones.

Each of these milestones is a particular point along the path of your practice development.

> A satisfied customer is the best business strategy of all.
>
> **Michael LeBoeuf**

As you create your successful practice, you are at a particular point along the path and look to get to the next point. However, the path is never straight and the distance between the points is always different.

How do you get from one point to the next?

You need a strategy. In fact, you need several strategies, one for each area of your practice:

- product development
- sales
- marketing
- financial

- administration/personnel
- IT
- clinical/operations.

Each of these strategies is described separately in the relevant parts of this book.

When you have a strategy, you avoid missing opportunities and make sure you achieve your action plans.

Setting up a strategy for each practice area shows you the alternative ways of moving to the next point and helps you realise your vision and mission.

08 Create a Great Patient Journey

And get more business as a result

Many dental practices treat each patient visit as a routine affair.

Make an appointment, come in, receive treatment, pay and go.

Big mistake!

Every single patient visit is your opportunity to make a lasting impression.

If you create a good impression, they're likely to come back.

If you create a totally memorable impression, they'll definitely come back. Plus they'll recommend you to their friends and family as well.

Treat each visit as a patient journey. A journey that, when handled properly, produces a 'wow factor' that creates stories and increases recommendations to your practice.

> According to the Harvard Business School, there is only one key measurement in business: How likely are patients to refer others to your practice, on a scale of 1–10? If 9–10, you've got a great practice.
> If less than 9, you're not working hard enough on the patient journey.

The journey for a new patient starts with the enquiry phone call. It then moves on to:

- how the enquiry is dealt with
- what literature is sent through the post
- what information is available on the website
- the patient walking through the door for the first time.

The patient journey continues right to the end, when treatment is complete and a follow-up phone call is made to ask how they're feeling.

Don't underestimate the importance of ongoing patient retention.

A dental practice in Dubai won a Best New Business Customer Service Award due to the excellence of the patient journey it provides.
How do they do it?
Partly by spending a lot of money on the practice to create a good impression. But also through the smaller points and attention to detail.
Some impressive plants outside the entrance to the practice, for example, were suffering due to the extreme heat. Rather than dig them out, a notice, signed by the dentist, apologised for their poor condition and explained how attempts were being made to grow them.
This level of attention gives a good impression of the practice and of the level of care patients can expect to receive.

How do you create the perfect patient journey?

A good way to start is to have a brainstorming session with your team.

Analyse every step of the patient journey. Aim to build in excellence at every point, supported by your systems and each member of your team.

You may want to include other services, such as dental spas and skin treatments; anything that will include the wow factor to make the patient journey more memorable.

Patient journey = wows = stories = raving fans = more recommendations

The patient journey is crucial to the success of your practice. Get it right and patients return again and again. And they bring others with them. This is the best marketing possible and best growth area for your business.

See Appendix B on page viii to see how a patient journey provides value.

09 Mission Accomplished

The importance of celebrating your successes

> However beautiful the strategy, you should occasionally look at the results.
>
> *Winston Churchill*

Setting goals is vital but celebrating when you achieve them is just as important.

As outlined previously, you need to set both personal and business goals. This gives you targets to aim for. And if you hit those targets, you must celebrate every achievement.

Record each goal and then track it so you can measure the progress you make.

Check what you have achieved every 12 months. This can be at the end of the year or at the anniversary of setting your goals.

If you pay off a debt, improve income as planned or assemble your team, that's a success. Ensure you mark all your achievements with a milestone celebration.

Make a point of celebrating every single success. It's something else to work for and to which you can look forward.

Celebrate the achievement of a goal before moving on to the next one.

Many practices don't set goals. They simply concentrate on the surgery and patients. In doing so, they finish up on a treadmill, working from day to day with no special occasions to anticipate.

Celebrations don't have to be lavish affairs but it's important you do something. Share the achievement of personal goals with a meal for family and friends.

Mark hitting business targets with a team member of the month award so those who contribute to the success can share in the celebration.

Whatever you do, do something.

And while you must celebrate a success, don't treat the failure to achieve a goal as a tragedy. Instead, establish what went wrong and change your strategy so you hit the target next time.

Team Building

If you want to achieve all your aims for the practice, you must have all members of the team behind you.

Without their support, you'll fail.

The following chapters tell you how to ensure they come with you on the journey.

10 Choose the Right Business Structure

The need for regular board meetings

If you've got a small dental practice, holding board meetings might seem a little over the top.

Well it's not.
Every dental practice, no matter how small, must hold regular board meetings. And 'regular' means how often is necessary to deal with the business in hand. Monthly is usually too frequent, three–four times a year is about right.

Wondering why you need board meetings?

Because you need to focus on the strategies set up to achieve your vision, mission and personal goals.

You need to assess the progress on each of the strategies for your seven business areas described in Chapter 7 (product development, sales, marketing, financial, administration/personnel, IT and clinical/operations).

A board meeting is a way of communicating what is happening in the practice.

The point of having an official board meeting is it creates a corporate structure and establishes responsibility.

If you find it difficult or unnecessary to organise a physical meeting, have a 'virtual' board meeting, held online with participants in different locations.

But do ensure you have a meeting.

Attendees are those responsible for the seven areas of your practice.

You may also involve non-executive consultants whose job is to ensure you, as Principal, do not deviate from the vision and mission. They should also challenge you on action plans and opportunities that arise in the marketplace.

Their main purpose is to ensure the practice is constantly brought back to its core values, vision and mission.

Always hold board meetings at a specific time of day and, if possible, off-site so there are no interruptions. Each meeting must:

- be properly structured with an agenda
- officially sign off the minutes of the last meeting
- have minutes taken
- establish action points on the seven areas to ensure required actions are carried out
- set a date for the next meeting.

A typical agenda for a board meeting is:

1. Approval of the minutes for the previous meeting.
2. Managing Director's report – opportunities arising, what has been achieved, who has joined and left the team.
3. Progress and update of the overall strategy.
4. Reports on the individual seven strategies (people attending will be held accountable for the strategies and assigned actions).

By discussing the relevant parts of the practice at a formal board meeting, you are more likely to achieve the practice's vision, mission and core values.

11 Set the Roles

Get the right organisational structure for your practice

A dental practice typically comprises:

- a husband and wife partnership
- a Practice Manager
- a Business Manager
- external consultants and non-executives.

As Principal, you have the most responsibility.

In addition to handling the high-profile work, you run the practice, market it, aim to increase sales and so on.

You are generally supported by:

- self-employed associates who undertake specific work and are paid a percentage of revenue after deducting certain costs
- therapists, hygienists and vocational trainees who also work with patients.

Since associates are self-employed, they may not be team players. They may not sign up to your vision, mission and core values. Because of this, it's important you have a proper structure.

Everyone needs to know where they fit within the structure and to whom they report.

They have to be accountable to you as the Principal or to the Practice Manager or Business Manager. This is essential, if only to ensure the practice is properly resourced during holidays and at other times.

It's possible your organisation structure covers several sites to ensure they operate efficiently.

It's important that your organisation structure:

- is established and visible so everyone knows it

- satisfies the needs of your practice

- identifies the responsibility of each role and what the person in the role is accountable for

- evolves to meet changing circumstances.

> Create the best structure

Consider the following organisational structures and how they will affect you:

Version 1

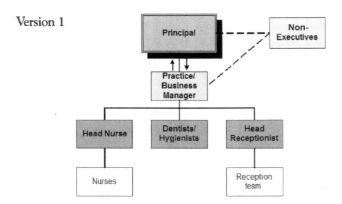

This is the best structure.

All communications flow through the Practice Manager or Business Manager to the Principal, who can concentrate on the vision and mission. However, dentists and hygienists may not be happy about not being able to communicate directly with the Principal.

Version 2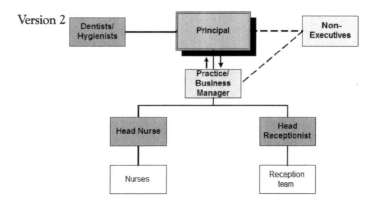

This structure addresses the concerns of the dentists and hygienists, who now report directly to the Principal.

This increases the load on the Principal, although most information still flows through the Practice or Business Manager.

Version 3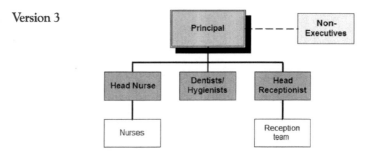

Here too many people report directly to the Principal, who is overloaded with information coming from all directions.

This may result in little time to devote to the vision and mission.

Get the structure right – it is vital for the success of your practice.

Equally important is ensuring people are in the correct roles. For this, you need personality profiling.

12 Round Pegs in Round Holes

Use personality profiling to ensure people are in the right roles

Everyone has strengths and weaknesses.

Know what they are and you can build a more effective team. You can put people in roles to which they are most suited and can provide training to address their weaknesses.

Personality profiling uses the 'DISC' acronym to measure natural characteristics:

- Dominance (generally a characteristic for a Managing Director)
- Influence (Sales Director)
- Supporting (Human Resources Director)
- Compliance (detail person)

Where do you fit in?

If you're a typical dentist, you've probably got good people and detail skills. Chances are you aren't particularly dominant but are reasonable on the sales side.

If you're not naturally dominant, you need support to take the practice forward.

If you do have a high 'D' rating, try to devote a day a week to the organisation and running of the practice. Alternatively, appoint a Business Manager to handle it for you.

If you don't like to discuss fees, appoint a Treatment Coordinator (with a high 'I' rating). This person can then handle the sales side of the practice.

> Get the right mix

When you're holding board meetings, you ideally need a mix of people to make it work:

- a Creator to put forward ideas and suggestions
- an Implementer to put ideas into practice
- a Destroyer who will identify elements to get rid of ideas that won't work.

You need a combination of idealists and realists for an effective board that helps you lead as Managing Director. If you're all creators, you'll have great ideas but nothing will ever get done.

To ensure you've got people in the right roles, run a programme of personality profiling. Each profile can be done online and takes around 10 minutes.

Start with yourself as Principal plus other key people. The aim is to assess strengths and weaknesses, matching them against each participant's role.

If profiling identifies a missing skill set, bring in a non-executive person to fill the gap. If you're low on dominance as a board, appoint a non-executive chairperson.

When financial skills are low, recruit an accountant. The external person is sometimes just a facilitator who encourages discussion and makes things happen and keeps you from deviating from your path.

Once you sort out all the weaknesses, you have a more complete team to take your practice forward.

13 Run a Team Day

How this helps build a genuine team spirit

A crucial event in your business calendar is an annual Team Day, which the whole team must attend.

The aims of the day are to explain what you're trying to achieve and to get the team involved. It's vital each person feels part of the team and can make a contribution to the practice success.

Like board meetings, ensure the Team Day is properly structured and planned. Set out everything you're going to cover on a flipchart or use a presentation application.

See Appendix C on page x for a sample Team Day agenda.

Point one on the agenda is for you to deliver your vision and mission to the team. Explain why you are passionate about both.

If some parts of your vision are too personal, leave them out. But cover the main points to get your message across.

Once you set out your clear vision and mission, allow time for your team to discuss them. Split the team into groups of two or three so they can decide whether they like everything you've said.

It's important you allow your team to challenge your vision and mission so they feel part of the process. Each discussion group can appoint a spokesperson who may challenge you on certain points.

As a result of discussions and the ensuing challenges, be prepared to change some elements if the consensus is against them.

The more passionate and realistic you are in delivering your vision and mission, the less likely you are to be seriously challenged.

Once you complete the vision and mission, the next agenda item is to present your core values. Again, allow challenges and be prepared to make changes.

> Encourage suggestions

Some time before the Team Day it's a good idea to ask team members to suggest five things they'd like to change in the practice. These can be sent in advance to the person running the meeting, who presents the points in priority order.

Be prepared for criticism, common complaints of dental practices being:

- communications are poor
- associates aren't team players
- the Principal says and starts a lot but doesn't complete much.

What you do is ask your team their opinions, give them their say and find out what they think is wrong in the practice. When they split into groups, ask them to discuss the points raised and suggest ways of improvement.

You have to be prepared to listen to what is said and take some action as a result of the suggestions.

If you do, the outcome is your people will feel genuine members of the team and they 'buy into' your plans.

14 Team Buy-in

Make sure everyone pulls in the same direction

The aim of the Team Day is to get team buy-in to the vision, mission and business goals of your practice.

It's vital you get the whole team behind you and they believe in what you're trying to achieve. Each member knows where the practice is going, has their say and feels their opinions are valued.

Once you achieve team buy-in, explain the organisational chart so everyone knows where they are in the structure and to whom they report (see page 46). Also emphasise where there are opportunities for growth.

Think of your team in sporting terms.

The Principals are the attackers, the Practice Manager and Head Nurse make up the midfield and the rest are defenders.

If the defenders don't do their jobs, the midfielders have to drop back to help out. This means they can't provide a service for the attackers. When the attackers don't perform correctly, other gaps appear.

The attackers need the assistance of the midfielders and the defenders if they are to score goals. You want the defenders to defend but also to support the midfield. This allows the midfielders to go forward and help the attackers.

All the players must understand the strategy and the tactics. If they don't, the team can't operate properly.

It's the same in business. If everyone doesn't operate as part of the team, your practice will not prosper and may not even survive.

You may find that certain team members are not happy making the changes necessary to achieve the goals you share with them. They may subsequently choose to leave. It is important that you allow them to do this if you are to achieve your vision and live your life as you want to live it.

Getting team buy-in is vital to the success of your practice. Achieve it and everyone is committed to the cause. Fail and you run the risk of people pulling in different directions.

Performance Management

Setting out your aims is all well and good, but you need to know if you achieve them.

You must know how well you're doing so you can plan ahead. Here you will learn how to manage and measure your performance.

15 Measure Performance

Involve your team to get the best outcome

Creating a successful dental practice requires you to set your vision, mission, core values and business goals; then celebrate each success as you achieve it.

How do you measure success?

Some measurements are relatively easy.

If you have to complete a set value of Units of Dental Activity (UDAs) to fulfil your NHS contract, just record each unit as it is completed. Then measure progress each month to ensure you hit the target by the end of March. Similarly, measuring recall rates and budgeting is relatively simple accounting.

If a vision is to achieve team happiness, that's more difficult to measure. How do you know who's happy and who's not?

One way is to have a mood board where each team member can record their happiness level that day. Another is a weekly email that indicates each person's state of mind.

The challenge is to express the vision, mission and the rest in words.

The best way to establish measurements is involve your team. This has several advantages. It:

- gets several viewpoints on the problem

- gives each member the opportunity to challenge the aims and measurements

- ensures the team buys into the aims and their measurements.

You generally have a Vision Day early in the process to create your vision. Around four weeks later, have a Team Day to set your measurements.

Organise your team into groups of two or three and ask each group to look at your vision, mission, core values and goals. Have them convert the words into measurements that can be applied.

The outcome of this activity is a One Page™ Plan, described in the next chapter. By involving your team in the creation of this plan, you get buy-in on its aims and the measurement of success.

> Measurement aids

To help you set your measurements, a number of forms are provided in Appendix D:

SWOT worksheet (see page xi) to undertake a SWOT analysis of the practice. This identifies:

- Strengths, which may include the quality of your team

- Weaknesses, such as the inability to convert NHS patients to private patients

- Opportunities, perhaps bringing in consultants to improve performance

- Threats, which could include changes to the NHS contract

Small business success questionnaire (see page xii), completed by the Principal. Scores below 6 indicate action is needed to improve the way the practice operates.

KickStart questionnaire (see page xvi), for all members of the management team. Scores below 60 are action points.

If scores relating to the practice differ, ask each respondent why they have scored at that level and try to rationalise the scores.

Reverse appraisal form (see pages xix–xxi) provides each team member's view of the Principal. The results indicate where improvement is needed in communication, planning, conflict resolution, etc.

16 Use the One Page™ Plan to Control Progress

You establish how you measure performance so you can produce a One Page™ Plan.

Produce a version of the plan each year to provide a summary of aims. It sets out where you are now and where you want to be in one year's time.

Each plan will vary, depending on what you want to achieve. A sample plan is shown next:

January XX			
XYZ Practice			
The latest update to our One Page™ Plan for the year ended March XX			
Key Results	Actual	Target	Comments
Profit			
Turnover			
New Patients			

Key sales drivers	Target/ Actual	Key actions	Key cost & cash drivers	Key actions
No. referrals from patients	TBA/	Run list from software each month	Profit	
No. new patients	30/	Target xxx per year No. where from/ value to be measured each month	Turnover	
No. patients lost	0/	Run report re. deregistered patients each month	Debtors	
No. patients lost regretted	0/	No. who left for a reason and were regretted - each to get a letter from x	Costs above budget - no. of instances	

% treatment plans converted	100%/	Calculate % figure of those who said yes vs total estimates
% converted treatment plans started within one month ("excellent service")	100%/	% of those who said yes and began treatment within the month
% patients who also saw hygienist in last month	100%/	Full list of patients vs those seeing hygienist
No. complaints	0/	
UDA target	1200/	

Value of bleaching	
Level of overheads	

Key underlying success drivers	Target/Actual	Key actions
Enhancing people's smiles	TBA/	
Patient happiness	TBA/	
Welcome systems	0/	
In-the-chair service touches in place	TBA/	
Post-treatment WOWs	n/a/	All patients after treatment of £1k value and above
Team study zone	X hours p.m./	One person per fortnight to read article and present at team meeting
No. new patient services	2/	
Ideas	x/	One idea per person per month. Ideas to be discussed at team meetings. Quarterly prize for team member with most ideas implemented
External team training	x/	Team to complete training matrix
Internal team training	x days p.a./	
Team happiness	5/	Weekly record of mood board taken on Weds. Average mood rating target = 5
Systems	x/	

Our Mission

Our Vision

The plan starts from the bottom with your vision and mission, working up to the expected key results. To achieve these results, various drivers are listed with the actions needed.

Target values are shown for each driver, with space to record the actual outcome.

All drivers have systems and team names behind them.

The assigned people own their particular figures. They are responsible for running the appropriate systems and reporting the actual outcomes.

17 Schedule Team Meetings to Establish Communications

One of the tasks within a Team Day (described in Chapter 13) is to agree communication structures within the practice.

Communications can take many forms and you choose whatever meets your needs. Examples include:

10-minute huddle – an informal meeting, generally at the start of each day. Points discussed include:

- good and bad systems and events from the previous day

- today's events (new and existing patient visits)

- any other business related to work.

Weekly communications meeting – involves everyone. This covers:

- what is happening in the coming week

- any gold patients (see Chapter 30) due to visit

- the general flow of patients over the week.

Monthly/fortnightly team meeting – the whole team discuss progress against the One Page™ Plan (see Chapter 16) and the project plan (see page xx).

Monthly/fortnightly Principal and Practice Manager meeting – covers key issues (such as revenue failings, cash flow shortages and team illnesses).

Monthly/fortnightly dentists and hygienists meeting – discusses clinical cases and conducts peer reviews.

Monthly/fortnightly nurses and receptionists meeting –deals with projects affecting the nursing or reception teams.

Quarterly board meeting – see Chapter 10.

Annual Team Day – see Chapter 13. This is mainly team building but you can also discuss any relevant issues. If your vision includes a phrase such as 'great or excellent service', stage the day in a top-class restaurant to provide experience of the service level and allow feedback.

Ensure every meeting is scheduled in the diaries of everyone who attends. Any meetings, other than the daily team huddle, must have proper minutes with action points set for those responsible.

> *Report every outcome*

An important outcome of each meeting is action points. These include actions to take in connection with the measurements in the One Page™ Plan.

Set up a project plan so you can keep track of what needs to be done. This can be a spreadsheet file (such as Excel) with a worksheet for each of the seven business areas (product development, sales, marketing, financial, administration/personnel, IT and clinical).

On each worksheet, record details of every project within the business area, covering:

- a description of the project
- action required
- the person responsible for the action
- when it is due for completion.

It's a good idea to colour code each project so its status is immediately obvious:

- **red** when not started
- **amber** while in progress
- **green** once complete.

Most importantly, ensure project plans are available to those who need to see them. This may be everyone.

Post them on the practice intranet, in the team room or kitchen. Just make sure people know where they can see them.

18 Spread the Load with a Good Practice Manager

Never underestimate the value of a good Practice Manager.

The Practice Manager:

- is one of the most important people in any dental practice

- implements the strategies necessary to achieve your vision and mission

- upholds the core values of the practice

- gives direction to and gets the best performance out of your team

- deals with project plans

- implements and upholds systems

- is involved with the financials and the measurement of the practice.

As Principal, your Practice Manager will be your right-hand person. He or she will lead your practice labour (costing maybe around £250,000 annually). You must, therefore, ensure you have the best person in place.

Think back to the sporting analogy in Chapter 14 (see page 54). The Practice Manager is the midfield and so provides the link between the defenders and the attackers. Similarly, in terms of the bus driver example in Chapter 6 (see page 35), the Practice Manager is the bus conductor who ensures everyone on the bus is there and sits in the right places.

Having a good, tight relationship with your Practice Manager will ensure your practice thrives.

Organisation structure version 1 in Chapter 11 (see page 47) is the best arrangement since all information flows through the Practice Manager to you. This reduces the burden on you so you can do more clinical work and increase revenue.

Some Practice Managers have been in the job for a long time and are resistant to change. Sometimes these people prefer to leave rather than introduce anything new. Principals are often reluctant to confront their Practice Managers in these circumstances but it has to be done.

Your Practice Manager must be in tune with your plans and needs because their involvement is essential if you are to achieve success.

> Get the Practice Manager you need

A Practice Manager is sometimes an ex-nurse who has moved up the career ladder. Such a person obviously has the benefit of practice experience but needs training in skills such as human resources, project planning and financial matters.

Conversely, there are moves to employ Business Managers who will have skills in human resources, marketing and other business aspects but need to gain dental experience.

Depending on the size of your practice, you may employ a Practice Manager, Business Manager or both. This person(s) is/are key to the practice. I have seen salaries from £22,000 to £45,000 a year. You need to make the right choice depending on experience.

Ensure they have the correct personality profile (see Chapter 12) to fit in with the practice and its structure. Since they are fundamental to the practice, test for the appropriate skills in the interviewing process.

A typical Practice Manager job description is shown in Appendix E (see page xxiii). Ask questions that are relevant to the job description to ensure suitability.

You can filter out some unsuitable candidates by putting questions online. These are completed by applicants in order to profile them. Those scoring below a set percentage need not be interviewed.

The chosen Practice Manager has to gain the respect of the team. They are involved with every meeting and important decisions, so it's vital you make the correct choice.

19 Systemise Your Practise

How to get everything running smoothly

Systems are the difference between a practice that potters along and one that runs like a well-oiled machine.

You need systems set up for every part of your practice – product development, sales, marketing, financial, administration/personnel, IT and clinical.

Systems determine how everything operates in each area and in different circumstances. They ensure the practice runs smoothly, even if key team members are absent, because everything is set down.

Systems not only improve your practice performance, they also increase its value. Consider the following:

Business valuation survey

Imagine you have just inherited a large amount of money and want to spend some of it buying a practice. After doing a lot of research, you have found three practices that interest you. They all provide the same treatments and sell the same products. They are all the same size and they are all based in the same town.
But, as you will see, they differ in one very important way.

Business A
This practice has the same basic systems as everyone else in the industry. But like the rest of the industry, most of what it does is not systemised. And, if key people aren't around, some things don't get done well (and sometimes they don't get done at all!). As a result, the practice owner works 47.5 hours a week (which research shows is exactly average for the owner of a UK small business). And by working hard like that every week, he just about manages to take four weeks' holiday a year. In other words, it is a typical and very average small business.
This practice has been independently valued at £100,000 – which is an amount you can easily afford.

Business B
This practice has no systems at all. The practice owner has to drive everything. And, as a result, he works 60 hours a week sorting out problems, covering for absent team members, fighting fires and making things happen. He never seems to have time for things like planning since he is always busy working on more urgent things. And he only manages to take two weeks' holiday a year – when he spends the whole time worrying about how everyone will be coping without him!
This practice has not been independently valued. So, given that Business A was worth £100,000, how much would you be prepared to pay for this business?

Write your answer in the box

Business C
This practice has systems for everything. Those systems contain everything everybody needs to know to run the practice effectively and profitably. They are also continuously tested and improved. And everybody knows exactly what they are and how they work. So everybody uses them. As a result, the practice owner usually works only 35 hours a week, spends a lot of time on the golf course and in the gym, and took six weeks' holiday last year (when he didn't worry once about the practice – because he knew it would work perfectly without him).
This practice has not been independently valued either. So, given that Business A was worth £100,000, how much would you be prepared to pay for this practice?

Write your answer in the box

Your practice
Now imagine a scale of 1–200. And imagine on that scale...
Business B – the one with no systems at all – has a score of 1
Business A – the one with basic systems – has a score of 100
Business C – the fully systemised one – has a score of 200
What score on a scale of 1–200 would you give your practice?

Write your answer in the box

Why are systems important?

Set up good systems and you can:

- ensure everyone knows how to run the practice
- put your team in charge
- free your time as Principal
- step back if you wish
- test new ideas before you put them into practice
- replicate and grow your business
- increase your practice value (by an average of 86.77% according to research).

> Develop the best systems

Each set of systems covers a different part of your practice:

- Quality systems may deal with the prevention of cross-infection.
- Service systems define how to meet and greet patients, how to talk to people in the surgery, how to prevent lost business.

A receptionist, for example, has to undertake certain tasks and may require a cashing-up system and daily procedures.

Systems are unique to your practice and depend on your vision and mission. Each system is set out in a procedure manual, accessible through an organised file structure. Everyone knows how to find what they need.

The manuals describe how each system works. They contain set procedures that describe, for example, how to deal with incoming post or to meet and greet patients correctly.

Each person's job description has relevant systems linked to it. The person then reads and signs off the appropriate system descriptions.

Setting up systems and ensuring they're correctly filed isn't enough. Problems occur when:

- teams aren't following systems and inconsistencies occur
- systems are no longer accurate and need updating.

Appoint a Systems Champion tasked to get the practice systemised without delay. Once this is done, the System Champion ensures all systems are constantly up to date and followed. Any that are not working as they should are reported at Team Days.

If this seems a little involved, I assure you it needn't be.

So how do you get your systems developed?

You could do them yourselves, using your own resources. However, this is likely to be a long and frustrating experience.

A better way is to look for a 'leg-up' and utilise the experience of others.

One way of doing this is using software such as System BuilderTM. This software tool enables you to create your own systems using preset templates and forms.

The outcome of using the software is a system manual for the different parts of your practice. Although the operational systems are specific to your practice and need to be written, much of the rest may well be standard and require little adaptation.

Setting up systems quickly and effectively ensures your practice runs much more smoothly.

You also end up with a practice that's worth almost twice as much as before.

20 Get Results Through Accountability and Responsibility

Setting everything up is fine. But people need to be accountable to ensure results follow.

Once you ...

- have the systems required to achieve your vision and mission
- have measurements in place so you know when things are achieved
- have your overall project plan in place
- have names assigned to drivers in the One Page™ Plan

... you can attach systems and plans to job descriptions.

This makes each team member accountable for the appropriate systems, measurements and projects associated with their role. Tying all this in with appraisals ensures team members are keen to achieve their goals.

When you handle the accountability and responsibility correctly, most things get done without too much persuasion.

Financial

The previous section told you how to build your practice in the image you want. If you apply all the principles, you know where you're going and how you're going to get there.

In this section, we deal with the financial aspects of the practice.

You determine the business structure that best meets your needs, decide on the money you want to earn and learn how to ensure everything stays on track.

You end up with a practice that is as profitable, cost-effective and tax-efficient as you can make it.

The aim is more income without more effort.

21 Choose the Right Business Structure

Consider the best for you

Businesses in the UK vary in structure. You need to choose the one that's best for your practice.

The structure you choose may not impact on the day-to-day running of the practice and so may not seem crucial. However, it affects your relationship with the practice, the records you have to keep and, ultimately, the amount of taxation you pay.

Any decision you make is not set in stone and you can transfer to a different business structure if your practice grows or changes in nature. But this will take time, effort and money so it's best to get it right at the outset.

These are the most common business structures for dental practices.

- Sole trader is the simplest form and generally suitable for the smallest practice. You have complete control of the practice and receive all profits after paying income tax. However, you are responsible for all losses and liabilities, which means your personal property is at risk.

- Partnership applies when two or more people jointly own the practice. You share the management of the practice as well as the profits, risks and liabilities. Only form partnerships with people you trust and who will add value to the practice.

- Expense sharing partnership is specific to dentistry and other medical sectors. It applies when an associate or new partner buys into a partnership to gain a share of the profits and additional job security. This is not a full partnership but most overheads are shared.

- Limited liability partnership removes some of the risks since the partnership has a distinct legal personality and the liability of each partner is limited to a set amount. Additional filing and disclosures are required although each partner is still taxed directly.

- Limited liability company ensures the practice is a distinct legal entity that is separate from its owners, whose liability is limited to the value of the shares they own. Large businesses are often public limited companies with their shares quoted on the Stock Exchange.

Whichever type you choose, you need to balance risk and restrictions against financial considerations. It's always best to seek legal advice so you don't make a mistake. One of the best specialist dental lawyers is John Grant of Cohen Cramer, based in Leeds – see www.cohencramer.co.uk.

You must be sure to tie up all legal aspects. In particular, the NHS contract must be written into the appropriate trading vehicle as well as the associates' contracts, and employment contracts must be up to date.

Set up a proper structure and you have a working arrangement for your practice. However, gain agreement with all interested parties — in the form of a partnership agreement or shareholders' agreement.

It's also essential there are provisions for deadlocks or should relationships break down. There has to be an agreed buying-out process, appropriate insurance in place and cover for all eventualities. This ensures the practice survives even if a partnership does not.

22 Model Building

Hit your income targets with the right business model

The business structure defines your practice as a legal entity.

The business model you adopt is in many ways much more important. It determines the services you offer, how they are provided and, ultimately, the profitability of your practice.

Consider the example business structure set out when discussing your business goals (see Chapter 5):

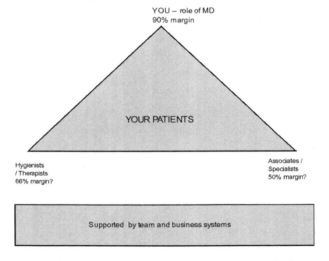

The amount and type of work you do determine the level of revenue the practice earns. Added to this, the way you resource this work sets the level of profitability for the practice.

A lot of this comes down to how you, as Principal, want to work.

You may do five days a week on private work such as implants. But if you devote a day a week to NHS work, revenue can be reduced.

Overall practice revenue is influenced by:

- how long the Principal works
- the type of work undertaken
- daily rate and growth
- number of holidays taken
- how many patients are seen each day.

For example:

$$£2,500 \text{ per day x } 4.5 \text{ days a week x } 45 \text{ weeks a year}$$
$$= £506,250 \text{ target gross revenue}$$

As Principal, you are the highest earner. Consequently, you should handle all:

- gold and silver patients (see Chapter 30)
- patients with potential for new work
- new patients
- specialist work.

Associates will deal with the rest of the work, including NHS contacts.

If you have an NHS contract, set monthly UDA targets to ensure you hit the annual target. Also set targets for associates, both for NHS and private work, so you achieve your revenue needs.

> Get the right mix

Once you know the type and amount of work you're going to be doing, you decide how it's going to be resourced. This decision has a massive impact on your level of profitability.

Consider the following:

Fees	£1 million	£1 million	£300,000	£300,000
Profit	£40,000	£350,000	£60,000	£130,000
Net profit %	4%	35%	20%	43%

Why are these figures so different?

This is a combination of two reasons:

- the type of work that's undertaken (private work is more profitable than an NHS contract)
- how you resource and pay for the work.

By restructuring your practice, you can achieve significant increases in profitability. Here's a real-life example:

- Restructuring a 60% NHS practice (£330,000 UDA contract value)
- Turnover £550,000 per year, costs £470,000, profit £80,000
- Limited company
- Two directors – one works four days a week and the other three days a week
- One employed associate on a £60,000 annual salary
- Two years later – turnover £620,000, costs £400,000, profit £220,000

Some of this is achieved by undertaking work that is more profitable. However, you gain significant improvements when you take work in-house and ensure it is carried out in the most cost-effective manner.

Ideally, provide every service you offer in-house. The only exceptions are the more complex cases that don't occur often enough to generate regular income.

When you provide nearly all services in-house, you:

- make more profit for the practice
- enhance the goodwill value of the practice
- create a good patient journey since patients only need to attend one location.

Here are some examples:

Implants

When you refer all implant work to an external specialist, one a month @ £2,500, this is worth £30,000 a year.

A 15% rental fee will generate £4,500 annual revenue or £45,000 over 10 years.

You can make more money by having the specialist handle the implant itself while you deal with the crown. A fee of £900 per crown will generate £108,000 over 10 years before laboratory fees.

Or ask a specialist to become an associate and this would generate £150,000 based on 50% pay.

Hygienists

Typically:
- £90–130 per hour charge rate
- £25–35 hourly cost

This gives averages of:
Charge £110 – Cost £35 = Profit £75
Gross profit = 68%
If:
- number of active private patients = 1,000
- 90% of them should see the hygienist = 900
- number of active patients seeing hygienist = 450
- potential patients to see hygienist = 450

Therefore:
- 2 @ 30 minutes per year = £110 income/£75 profit per hour
- Potential profit is 450 patients x £75 = £33,750 per annum

In-house hygienists provide a good gross profit as long as there is a reasonable volume of patients using their services and a good rate of recalls and internal referrals from the dentists.

Other specialist services

Whilst root canal work can be brought in-house, this requires much specialist equipment. Feasibility and profitability therefore depends on payback time for capital equipment and the frequency of work.

Other services to consider bringing in-house are *dental surgery*, *sedation* and *maxillofacial surgery*. These can sometimes be handled on a split-fee basis to make the figures work out.

The problem with bringing orthodontic work in-house is treatment can take a long time and so profits are slow to come into the practice. Up-front payments help cash flow but treatment can still typically last 18 months:

£4,000 fee – £400 materials
= £3,600 net
Over 18 months, is £200 per month

An associate may be paid a percentage of the work done, such as a 50% up-front fee. However, it is better to pay them monthly since the associate may leave part-way through the treatment. Cover any liability in the associate's contract.

A certain volume of patients is necessary to make it worthwhile to bring orthodontics work in-house. Whilst large, up-front payments help cash flow, the associate has to be kept occupied.

It comes down to simple mathematics – identify the services you want to provide and then work out the best, most cost-effective and profitable ways to provide them.

> Pay the rate for the job

Once you've decided on the top model (the top of the triangle on page 32), the flow of work goes down to hygienists/therapists and to associates/specialists.

You need to get the payment structure right for these people to ensure a profitable and successful practice.

Although some may be employed by the practice, the normal arrangement is for them to be self-employed and covered by an associate's contract.

This typically pays them 50 per cent of fees less laboratory and other costs. However, due to additional costs from the Care Quality Commission and others, the model is changing.

Associates are now often paid on a sliding scale, such as:

- 40% on the first £10,000
- 45% on the next £2,500
- 50% above that level.

Paying 50 per cent after fees often translates into actual gross profit of around 30 per cent. If the primary care trust (PCT) pays you £25 per UDA, you may pay the associate £10.

Irrespective of this, it is essential associates are team players and buy into the practice vision, mission, core values and systems.

Always ensure you get the best value for money from your resources. Don't use highly paid team members to do work that can be done by those on lower remuneration.

For example:

- Vocational trainees, who have their salaries paid by the PCT, can help.

- Dental therapists are allowed to do dentistry apart from initial examinations. The best arrangement is often that dental therapists undertake dental work prescribed by dentists.

The trick to making your business model work is to ensure all parts gel together.

You must maximise growth in each area, take advantage of every marketing opportunity and push each patient service to its limit.

Set forecasts and targets in all areas and track actual results against them.

You achieve maximum revenue when associates refer work to hygienists, specialists and to the Principal who does the specialist work. Although many argue this is part of their job, part of their team activities, it may be worthwhile providing an incentive in the form of a referral fee.

If associates don't refer, they're likely to do the work themselves. This causes the work mix to go wrong, as the profit goes to the associate, the Principal gets little and overall profitability is reduced.

Set a target for referrals and display a board that illustrates actual achievement against target. Show, for example, the number of times:

- each dentist refers to a hygienist

- the hygienist actually converts the work (the patient had the work after referral).

This gives a system of accountability.

The percentage paid for referrals affects the profitability of the practice, cash flow and the achievement of your personal goals.

It's important, therefore, you keep track of what is paid out and the resulting income.

23 Build Capital Value Through Good Margins

The business model you establish directly affects the margins you earn.

It determines the gross margin and the overall profitability of your practice. Clearly, as the highest earner with the best margins, your role as Principal has a major influence on the figures.

If you don't work full-time, don't do high-value work and employ high-earning associates, net profit may be only 15–20 per cent. On this basis, the volume of business going through determines if the practice is profitable or even viable.

The net profit you earn has a significant effect on the goodwill value of the practice. It's important, therefore, that you get the business model and structure right. This determines the capital value on exit. So it is absolutely crucial to your long-term future and achievement of your personal goals (see Chapter 3).

Benchmarking is key to moving forward since it shows if you're getting the margin right.

You are invited to contact Clear Vision for a fuller set of benchmarks that are relevant to your specific situation.

24 Key Performance Indicators

Check how everything is going while you still have time to act

Key Performance Indicators (KPIs) make it easy to keep track of what is happening.

KPIs can be anything you want to measure that will help you control the performance of the practice. Actual daily or hourly rates, gross income per surgery, UDAs per day, value of debtors, cash receipts, laboratory fees and so on.

The purpose of KPIs is to keep your finger on the pulse of the practice.

Each one should be important, measurable and easily understood.

You should be able to see, immediately, when KPIs are not what they should be and when corrective action is needed.

Decide on the key measurements that show the true performance of the practice on a weekly or monthly basis. These need to be discussed, agreed and measured at the appropriate interval and put into the One Page™ Plan (see Chapter 16).

Typical KPIs for a dental practice are:

1. How many active patients do you have?
2. What is your examination recall rate?
3. What is your hygiene recall rate?
4. What is the hygiene concentration rate?
5. What percentage of your patients know about all of your services and treatments?
6. What is your treatment conversion rate?
7. What is your marketing ROI (return on investment)?

8. What is your profit per month per service?
9. How many new telephone enquiries per week and what percentage book for an appointment and convert to patients?
10. Patient feedback.

In most cases, your KPIs will be derived from your One Page™ Plan (see Chapter 16) after your Team Day discussions.

Actual results should be generated automatically through your management accounts (Chapter 27), which will show your actual performance against budget.

25 Incorporation or Not?

If you're not incorporated, your personal assets are at risk.

However, incorporation means more work and expense.

So how do you decide what's best?

Many dental practices start out with a sole trader business structure. However, as the practice grows, a different structure may be more suitable.

Up until recently, incorporation for a dentist was not an option. Now it is, with the only stipulation being that at least one director has to be registered with the General Dental Council.

Whether you incorporate or not isn't a straightforward decision. You need to sum up the various positives and negatives, which are basically as follows:

> **Incorporation positives:**
>
> 1. potential to save tax
> 2. goodwill payout – enhanced personal reward
> 3. liability can be limited
> 4. creation of a corporate structure
> 5. easier and cleaner exit route
> 6. team motivation
> 7. use bank funding received on goodwill to pay off debts or improve personal assets.

> **Incorporation negatives:**
>
> 1. more time needed to maintain efficient records
> 2. statutory requirements to be met
> 3. annual return to be prepared for the General Dental Council
> 4. NHS contract transferred to a limited company.
> 5. HMRC may question the valuation
> 6. NHS pensions on incorporation have to be watched.
> 7. Income protection may be affected.
> 8. Ability to get mortgages may be affected.

Review the situation an individual basis – the situation is never the same between two people or practices.

The best course of action is to have an incorporation assessment prepared by your accountant. This will:

- look at the potential value of goodwill taking into account other assets and liabilities

- assess the profitability of the practice and what value can be drawn out (for living expenses, debt repayment, etc.)

- calculate whether incorporation is worthwhile in terms of potential tax savings.

In essence, the decision may come down to the amount of tax that can be saved.

Consider the following real-life example:

> - Husband and wife partnership
>
> - Net profit £120,000
>
> - Incorporated business
>
> - Goodwill value £520,000
>
> - Will pay only 21% Corporation Tax for the next 10 years, saving nearly £100,000 in tax

> Check the tax and cash flow implications

If you incorporate, the new limited company buys the goodwill from you as sole trader.

Since this is a sale of capital, you will pay Capital Gains Tax in the appropriate tax year. This is at the rate of 10 per cent of the gain currently.

The effect is, in the first year after incorporation, you pay three taxes:

- Capital Gains Tax on the sale of the business
- Corporation Tax on the profit made by the practice
- final Income Tax due under the previous arrangement.

It is important, therefore, that you plan for these outgoings since they may have a significant impact on your cash flow.

The company owes the original sole trader or partners the money for the sale of the goodwill. This is held in a directors' loan account and is drawn out of the practice when cash flow permits.

For example:

> The company purchases the goodwill for £400,000 and Capital Gains Tax of £40,000 is paid plus a further £30,000 to cover personal taxes.
>
> This leaves a residue of £330,000. This amount is available to be drawn tax-free from the company.
>
> Assume profit in a year is £150,000. Corporation Tax of £30,000 is paid, leaving £120,000 available for drawings.
>
> Should £40,000 be drawn as dividends, a further £40,000 may be taken from the loan account, reducing the outstanding balance to £290,000.
>
> The loan account is repaid over a further seven years. Earnings are taxed at a Corporation Tax rate of 21% (due to reduce to 20% from 1 April 2011) rather than a combination of Income Tax and National Insurance.
>
> The saving is £100,000 over a seven-year period (the difference between 20% Corporation Tax and 40% for Income Tax and National Insurance).

Although incorporation almost certainly produces tax savings, the circumstances of the practice may change.

It is important you undertake a full assessment of the implications, preferably with the assistance of your accountant, before you reach a decision.

If you decide to incorporate, there is a process you have to go through to ensure you do everything properly. An incorporation checklist is provided at Appendix F (see page xxv) to help you complete all the necessary steps.

In particular, make sure:

- the PCT transfers the NHS contract to the new company

- your bank understands the process in respect of financing since there is the opportunity to borrow money against goodwill. This may be used to pay off debts or buy assets to achieve your personal goals

- you get appropriate legal advice to ensure contracts are transferred and there is continuity in the event of the death of a shareholder

- arrangements are in place to keep the accounting records and deliver the returns required after incorporation.

Incorporation imposes additional responsibilities and incurs extra costs. However, it can provide significant tax savings and reduce the risk of operating a practice.

26 Have a Proactive Accountant
Don't just wait for things to happen

Many accountants claim to be proactive on their website and in their marketing literature.

But is it truth or is it myth?

To be effective, to help you achieve your goals, you need a truly proactive accountant.

To be genuinely proactive, your accountant has to:

1. Start your accounts within six–eight weeks of the year-end.
2. Finish your accounts within 20 working days.
3. Provide a review of your personal and business tax payments.
4. Supply a financial forecast that sets out how you will achieve your personal goals.
5. Produce management accounts so you know what profit you are achieving each month.
6. Undertake tax planning to minimise your personal and Corporation tax bills.
7. Discuss your figures and look at growth areas. Schedule a monthly telephone call to coincide with a meeting between you and your practice manager.
8. Prepare an annual goodwill valuation for your practice once the accounts are complete.
9. Communicate, communicate, communicate.

Your accountant may also provide other services that help you operate more efficiently. These include training your practice manager or business manager to prepare management accounts, forecasts and cash-flow statements.

As your year-end approaches, your accountant should send you a scheduling letter.

This sets out when the figures are expected from you, when draft accounts will be prepared and sent out, the likely date of a meeting to discuss the accounts and when accounts will be sent out to you for signature.

The turnaround time (see Point 2 above) is measured from when your books are received to when the draft accounts go out to you.

Many accountants either don't measure this time or it is between 20 and 80 days. This is inefficient. You need to know when your accounts are coming, when payments on account are due, what tax is due and when.

You also need any items adjusted in your year-end accounts to be reflected in your management accounts.

Does your accountant publish their turnaround times? Clear Vision has turnaround times as one of its KPIs, which are displayed in the reception area.

Your accountant has to be held responsible for producing work promptly. Getting figures in good time will help you to see whether the practice is moving in the right direction.

27 Prepare Management Accounts to Get Up-to-date Figures

The traditional way of finding out how you are doing is to look at your annual accounts.

The trouble is, annual accounts are only produced once a year and often some considerable time after the year-end. Everything they tell you is out of date. If things are going wrong, it's too late to act.

What you need is immediacy. What you need is management accounts.

Producing management accounts is not a particularly complex process. Nevertheless, management accounts have to be accurate, timely and meaningful if they are to be of any use.

Your accountant can help you by:

- training your Practice Manager or Business Manager to produce management accounts using a suitable accounts package

- providing checklists to follow when preparing monthly management accounts

- educating you and your management team to understand management accounts and act on the figures

- 'health-checking' the monthly accounts after receiving copies on disk or by email

- telephoning and offering advice during a monthly management accounts meeting between you and your Practice Manager/ Business Manager.

In any business, you need to know at all times where you are, from a profit point of view.

Integrated dental practice software is available that logs the treatments you carry out and pulls the details into a management accounts function.

The structure of your management accounts must be sufficiently detailed so the software you use generates the relevant information.

This may include:

- gross revenue per individual team member
- gross revenue per surgery
- revenue by type of service and individual
- laboratory fees and other costs so the profit from each type of work can be seen (e.g. revenue from crown work = £1,000, laboratory fee = £200, margin = £800. If reported margins differ, this is either due to not billing at the full rate, misposting or timing differences).

Management accounts should show the margin for each associate and include NHS fees and other income.

KPIs (see Chapter 24) should be an automatic by-product of management accounts, which allows you to keep track of each one so you can assess and correct your practice performance.

See Appendix G on page xxviii for a management accounts example.

28 Forecasts and Funding

See where you want to be and how you're going to pay for it

Management accounts tell you what you've done whereas forecasts show what you plan to do.

Before you produce your management accounts, you need an annual forecast to compare against. Ensure the forecast allows for holidays and includes drawings to cover your personal goals, tax and living expenses.

A conventional forecast starts with turnover, deducts costs to determine profit and then takes out drawings. Clear Vision works the other way round.

The 'upside down' forecast

First, determine what you spend in a year (your drawings, to cover living expenses, holidays, fees).

Add in the money you need for your exit plan or to achieve your personal goals (such as buy-to-let costs).

This gives you the profit you must make after tax. This is your start point:

    Profit after tax
    + Tax
    + Overheads
    + Cost of sales
    = Turnover

This determines the annual revenue you need to generate to earn a living and achieve your goals.

The start point, therefore, is your personal expenditure plan, which affects everything that happens in the practice.

Once your forecast is produced, don't just forget it. It's a tool to keep track of how well your practice is performing.

Discuss variances between actual and budget values every month. Identify why they have arisen and, for adverse variances, take corrective action. Explanations of variances must be attached to the accounts.

At every board meeting or annual review, look at your personal goals and ensure you are achieving them. Any changes you make to these goals will filter down through the whole of the practice.

> Prepare your forecast

Start to prepare your forecast for next year the month before your year-end. You then have the forecast completed shortly after the year-end and can insert the correct opening bank balance, up-to-date cash flow and profitability, plus accurate tax and loan repayments for the year. Approve the forecast at your board meeting.

When preparing your forecast, ensure that:

- overheads for the year are broken down by specific categories
- any one-off expenditure (such as a new website development) is included
- labour costs include future pay rises (already agreed in appraisals) and any other resources needed
- variable costs (such as for hygienists) are based on forecast requirements
- capital expenditure is included for cash flow purposes
- turnover targets are set for each producer.

All costs included in the forecast must be controlled. For example, there has to be in-house responsibility for stock control and material buying, to improve stock rotation and obtain maximum benefit from buying deals (bulk buying, multiple quotations, etc.).

Since you use an 'upside down' forecasting technique, everything is based on turnover and you need to adjust this if it doesn't match forecast requirements.

So, how do you increase your turnover? There are seven main ways to do this:

1. Charge higher prices from the first day of your new accounting year.
2. Increase the value of your NHS contract (although there is a danger private patients may then transfer to the NHS).
3. Provide additional services to existing patients (such as more hygiene work).
4. Introduce new services for existing patients (for example, implants, orthodontics and Botox work).
5. Gain new patients.
6. Purchase goodwill from another practice (buy a patient list).
7. Reduce the amount of patients you lose by putting a robust patient education system in place.

If you meet your NHS targets and are doing well, you can apply to your PCT for a non-recurring contract to do more UDAs. Depending on the PCT's budget, you may subsequently be able to convert this to an annual contract.

It's crucial your forecast includes a short-term cash flow forecast. This is generally a 13-week rolling cash flow with all predicted receipts and expenditure included in the appropriate weeks.

Accurate and up-to-date forecasts are particularly relevant to your bank, which expects detailed information to cover the funding you have. Annual forecasts and management accounts are often prerequisites when obtaining funding.

> Funding

You have the opportunity to borrow against goodwill to obtain funding for the achievement of your personal and business goals. However, your bank needs to see the bigger picture to be confident the debt is serviceable and forecasts play a big part in this.

When you purchase equipment, do so in a way that maximises the tax relief you get.

Fund your purchase appropriately by lease or hire purchase to match your payments to the financial reward you stand to make from it.

Marketing

Many people confuse marketing and sales, treating them as the same when in fact they're quite different.

Marketing is about lead generation while sales is concerned with converting those leads into actual work.

New patients predominantly come from existing patients, the website, then other marketing activity.

The biggest cost is on your website and other marketing activity.

The patient journey is key to attracting new patients from existing patients (see page xx).

In this section, we cover how you go about marketing your practice. You learn about the different types of marketing and how to determine if it's successful.

29 Set the Marketing Strategy

Generate the leads needed for sales growth

The aim of marketing is to increase the revenue of your practice.

In order to market effectively, you need a strategy. This is produced annually, is written down and states the level of leads you will generate to achieve the required sales growth.

For example, if ...

> required growth is £100,000 and
> each converted lead produces £4,000 in annual revenue and
> every five leads convert into one sale

... then required leads for the year are:

£100,000/£4,000 = 25 sales x 5 = 125 leads

This is your target for the year and all marketing efforts are geared towards achieving this figure.

Your first stage is to measure what's currently happening – how many new patients come in and from what source. If you don't know where they come from, you can't follow them up properly.

Your marketing strategy covers:

- what you are going to do in terms of brand awareness and external marketing (Chapter 32) plus internal marketing (Chapter 33)

- what funds you require for the marketing budget

- who is going to do the work

- when the work is to be done

- systems required to achieve the desired leads

- any work that has to be outsourced

- what reporting mechanisms are needed

- how often marketing meetings are to be held

- who is in charge of the marketing strategy.

To be able to create your marketing strategy, you have to define your ideal patient (see the next chapter).

30 Identify Your Ideal Patient and Boost Your Revenue

Your ideal patient is one who is likely to generate most revenue for your practice.

Identify your ideal patient. It is crucial to the success of your marketing strategy.

Firstly, define the characteristics of your ideal patient, which may include:

- have a large family group
- are business people
- are within a certain age group
- manage their own health well
- are nice to deal with
- pay on time
- are likeable people
- have recommended to other patients
- are in the right location
- are well connected
- have had substantial work done or have the potential to do so.

Set out the preferred characteristics of your ideal patient. Then go through your existing patient base and score each patient by allocating Yes (5) or No (0) against each characteristic.

If you have a list of 8 characteristics, this will give a maximum score of 40 points. You can then categorise patients depending on their total score, for instance:

- 30+ points – gold

- 25+ points – silver

- 15+ points – bronze

- 10+ points – tin

- below 10 points – bin (that is, lose these patients if you feel inclined to do so).

Having categorised your patients, the ideal situation is that the Principal sees:

- all gold and silver patients

- those marked as having potential

- all new patients, then allocating them to other dentists depending on how they are rated

- those requiring specialist work.

Mark the patients with potential with an asterisk against their category (e.g. silver* or tin*). Make sure the Principal sees these patients and allow extra time for their appointments so there is the opportunity to discuss other treatment.

You can mark NHS or plan (monthly payment) patients with an asterisk too (i.e. NHS* or plan*) if they have the potential to go private. Again, allocate additional appointment time so the Principal can talk to them about going private or having some private work done.

Out of this exercise comes a marketing strategy aimed at attracting ideal patients to the practice. These are the patients that generate the most revenue.

31 Measure Return on Investment to See if Your Marketing is Effective

Marketing costs money.

To ensure your marketing is effective measure the return on investment (ROI) against every cost. For example:

- If a Yellow Pages entry costs £1,000 and generates one enquiry with no conversion to a sale, it's all cost with no return.

- If a £1,000 cost generates three enquiries and one conversion with £200 income in a year, you need five years of the same to get your money back on turnover alone. In terms of profitability, it will take even longer.

You need to look at the lifetime value from a profit point of view to see the true ROI. When you know the ROI, you know the effectiveness of marketing and can determine next year's marketing budget.

To measure the ROI accurately, you have to know where all your leads come from. Ensure that your receptionist asks each new patient where they heard of the practice. Then record this against the appropriate marketing cost in order to assess the ROI.

A marketing results log form is provided at Appendix H (see page xxx).

Ensure that your software system allows for the source to be identified as either the patient name or the marketing activity. Ensure the marketing activity is relevant to the expenditure you are currently spending to track the relevant ROI.

All other non relevant activities should be deleted so this will not give you the wrong results.

32 Brand Awareness

Get yourself known through external marketing

For a new business, brand awareness is key.

Setting up a practice and waiting for the patients to roll up just doesn't work. You have to let people know you're there and what you do.

You can get the word out in lots of ways – newspaper advertisements, leaflet drops, all sorts of things. If people know you're there, they come. If they don't, you might as well lock the doors.

External marketing can be handled through a combination of media:

- advertising in various publications
- attendance at events such as wedding fairs ('get the perfect smile for your big day')
- advertising board outside the premises and general signage
- website describing all available services
- sponsorship of local events
- Yellow Pages entry
- Internet pay-per-click.

External marketing is all about spending money to attract new patients.

33 Why Internal Marketing is Effective

Use it before looking further afield

With internal marketing, you're dealing with people you already know, so it's easier and more cost-effective than external marketing.

Internal marketing is all about asking your existing patients to bring you new patients. Consider the three different ways to ask them.

- Ask them to 'refer' others to your practice.

- Ask them to give personal 'recommendations' to others.

- Ask them to issue 'invitations' to others to visit your practice.

You may, for example, say to your existing patients you're expanding the practice. Give each of them a few cards they can use to invite family and friends to join the practice.

This is the best way to grow the practice, increase the value of the practice goodwill and add to the capital value. But you need a consistent system everyone follows, with all members of your team handing out the cards.

One thing to bear in mind is any new patients you get are likely to be of a similar type to those who refer them. Therefore, if you want more ideal patients, ask existing patients in the relevant categories to do the referring.

To make the whole exercise more effective, introduce a reward system to thank your patients for their efforts.

Every month, print off a list of the patients who have recommended others. Send each of these patients a handwritten, branded postcard from the Principal thanking them for their recommendations.

A key measurement in your One Page™ Plan (see Chapter 16) should be the sending out of thank-you cards. You may also create a reward system that provides free wine or a meal to the patients who make three or more referrals.

> Use your connections

If you have well-connected patients (identified by the categorisation exercise in Chapter 30), you may be able to help each other.

For example, if the patient runs a hairdressing salon, has a health spa or is a doctor, you may be able to run a joint marketing campaign and promote both businesses. You can also post advertisements in each other's premises for added publicity.

Schmoozing, or relationship marketing, pays dividends with the right kind of patient.

If you have twenty gold patients and four of them enjoy golf, hold a 'Dental Golf Day' and ask each of them to invite a friend. This has multiple benefits since you:

- are rewarding your gold patients
- are creating a story that may generate publicity
- may get four new gold patients.

You can do something appropriate for each category of patient:

- invite silver patients to a social evening
- send Christmas cards to your bronze patients.

In effect, you're providing a reward that matches the patient's category. The idea is that existing patients experience such a great level of service they become fans of the practice and refer other patients.

Have a 'schmoozing and thank-you budget' to cover the cost. Make your Practice Manager and receptionist responsible for capturing referral data and ensuring patients are adequately rewarded.

34 Existing Patients

Tap into the resources you already have

Not only do existing patients provide your current revenue, they are also a valuable resource in other ways.

Your patients are a potential source of additional work. Never miss an opportunity to market your services to existing patients because it's an easier process than starting afresh with new ones.

While a patient is in the surgery chair you can, as a result of a dental examination, give a dental score out of ten. Explain the reasons for the score and illustrate with a dental camera or mirror. The same applies for a hygiene score.

After giving your assessment, you can put forward recommendations to improve the score. You are, therefore, in control.

Ensure all your patients complete an evaluation questionnaire. This includes details of how they wish to improve their smile, appearance or other aspects.

Go through the options with before-and-after photographs or use software to show the benefits of a potential makeover.

Illustrate the effects of veneers, whitening or other treatments so the improvements are obvious. This is a really powerful marketing tool that makes a big impression on the patient.

It is the responsibility of every dentist to talk to their patients about treatments that can be offered. Additionally, the practice website, brochures and other literature should show all available services with before-and-after illustrations.

Another source of information for existing patients is the dental reception area. Have a screen with a loop display showing what a crown is, what root canal surgery involves and so on.

The purpose of the displays, website and other literature is to combine educational content with a wow factor. Patients see the benefits and are encouraged to have the treatment illustrated.

As well as providing all the necessary literature for your patients, speak to them about all available services.

There is little point spending money on external marketing if you don't make the most of your internal resources.

Unless you have a start-up practice, maximise the potential of your existing patients before you market externally.

35 Specialist Marketing

Build your relationship with dentists to obtain more referrals

If you don't run a general dental practice, your marketing challenges are altogether different.

You may operate purely as an orthodontist, implantologist or endodontist. If so, you survive by patient recommendations or referrals from dentists.

Patient recommendations come down to the level of service you give.

If you have a specialist practice and get many patient referrals, this is generally as a result of providing a high level of service and patient journey. Consequently, you justify higher fees and the practice is worth more.

Dentist referrals are a different matter because they depend on the relationship you have with each dentist. You therefore need to assess and nurture these relationships to keep the referrals coming through.

Specialist marketing is about measuring the amount of referrals you get from each dentist on a monthly basis.

You then categorise the dentists as gold, silver, bronze and tin depending on the number and quality of referrals you receive and the general situation.

Questions you use to categorise your dentists include:

1. Do we know all the dentists at the practice?
2. Do we know if any of the existing referrers are retiring?
3. Is there more potential to get other work from the referring dentists?
4. Are they in the right location?
5. Are they giving quality leads?

As with your patients (see Chapter 30), score 5 for each Yes answer and 0 for No. Then grade the dentists as gold, silver, bronze or tin based on the points scored.

Once you've completed the grading, put a contact system in place so, for example:

- the tins are seen once a year
- gold dentists are seen every two months.

Aim to educate the referring practices so they learn what you're about.

Specialists can go out to the referring dentists and explain to the whole team what they do and what is happening in their field. As a result, the team members increase their education and may earn Continuing Professional Development points.

Make sure you have a system in place so you speak to your referring dentists regularly. Take them out for meals, to football matches or, in exceptional circumstances, take them abroad to dental symposiums.

Relationship marketing can pay big dividends.

> Build a relationship

You will always be interested in new referrers as a source of work.

But concentrate first on maximising referrals from your existing referrers.

Some specialists have never met their referring dentists and sometimes don't even know who they are. This is a serious omission and an important part of relationship marketing is to get to know them.

You find ways of meeting referring dentists, you visit them and you build up a relationship. Only when you've done this do you target the other dentists in your area.

Finding new referrers involves cold marketing, which can mean you send out brochures, conduct e-marketing or any other suitable process. Before you can do this, build up a target list you can approach. You need to identify practices that may refer to a specialist.

This isn't necessarily a quick process. You have to identify practices in your area and decide which of them are potential sources of referrals.

Look at their websites and see what services they offer. If they provide orthodontist, implant and other services that match yours, they clearly won't refer the work to you.

Do some validation first and you avoid unnecessary cold marketing.

You market your practice as a specialist business with a view to getting referrals from dentists that don't provide the service you do.

When you get referrals, don't just take it for granted. Whenever you receive a referral, send an immediate thank-you letter.

You can also send progress letters to update the dentist with the status of treatment. After all, your referred patient is also the patient of the referring dentist, who will be keen to know what is happening.

You can even dictate a personal message and send the audio file as an email attachment. The referring dentist then hears you talking about his or her patient.

The whole purpose is to establish a good, long-term relationship with each dentist. You can then rely on a steady flow of high-quality work.

Sales

Selling is something most dentists don't like. They regard themselves as technicians, as service providers rather than sales people.

Selling is probably the most important activity in any dental business. What you really do is exchange a service you provide for money from the patient (or the NHS).

Think of it as 'treatment plan conversion' if it makes you feel better. We will continue to use sales.

This section outlines the sales strategy you should follow, what you do to make it work and how you determine if it's succeeding.

36 Get the Sales Strategy Right

Know what you want and how you're going to achieve it

Sales (or treatment plan conversion) is about converting leads into actual work.

Your leads are generated through marketing activities. However, they get no further unless you put in the effort.

The sales strategy you adopt is driven by a number of factors:

- What prices are you going to set and when?

- What additional services should you add to achieve your sales forecasts?

- What are the key sales systems your team needs to learn and improve on?

- What scripts and systems should your team use in order to make your treatment plans compelling?

The answers to these questions determine the features of your sales strategy.

37 Proper Training

The way to ensure effective sales conversion

To make your treatment plan conversion strategy effective, you need to ensure the right people are in place and are properly trained.

Do the dentists have the ideal personality profile for converting treatment plans?

Are they comfortable converting treatment plans?

Is an additional resource required to handle treatment plan conversion?

You may need to provide training for team members so they are familiar with using treatment plan conversion techniques. This type of training is available from various organisations, such as plan providers, consultants and patient finance companies such as Medenta.

If you have no one with a high 'I' factor (Influential, as described in Chapter 12), you may need to recruit.

Many practices employ a Treatment Coordinator, to discuss treatment options with patients. It's also important your nurses are trained in reception systems and conversely that the reception team is familiar with dental services. This transfer of knowledge can take place during daily team meetings.

There is a move to appoint reception personnel who are trained in customer service in hotels, retail establishments or the restaurant trade. This ensures they have great training in how to deal with customers but means they are lacking in dental knowledge. Whilst this can come later, it's essential your reception team is fully versed in dental matters.

38 Measure the Performance of Your Sales Strategy

Whatever treatment plan conversion strategy you establish, you measure the outcome to see if it's working.

Some key measurements are:

enquiries into reception from the website and other sources, including walk-ins:

- appointments booked

- enquiries converted to on-going patients

treatment plan conversion rate:

- how many plans are produced?

- how many plans are converted?

- at what value?

Look at the treatment plan follow-up process. A suitable software application will list incomplete treatments (where patients have a treatment plan but have not agreed to it).

All incomplete treatments must be followed up, either by a nurse, the Practice Manager, Treatment Coordinator or a dentist. The main decision is how soon after providing the plan before they are followed up.

39 Check Out the Opposition

Use a mystery shopper to see how others operate

No business operates in isolation and your practice isn't any different.

It helps to know how the opposition operates.

To aid the treatment plan conversion process, conduct a mystery shopper exercise. Use this to measure many features of the competition, including:

- the prices they charge
- how they answer the telephone
- the receptionists' knowledge
- whether brochures are offered and sent out
- how the website looks.

Undertake a mystery shopper exercise annually, before the start of your financial year. Two types are possible:

- via the telephone, when you can say you have just moved into the area and need a dentist
- via a physical visit when you pay a consultation fee.

The aim is to assess how well each practice performs in comparison to your own. You then take those lessons and use them to improve your level of service.

Here's an example of a mystery shopper exercise:

Asked by a client to visit an award-winning London practice.

Telephoned in June and first available new-patient appointment is September. Is this because they offer such a great service, because they're too busy or are too successful?

Exceptional literature sent through the post – very clear about the process, excellent testimonials, very good directions and information about finance plans.

On walking into the practice, receptionists spoke among themselves before realising they had a customer. Not great service.

Asked to take a seat. Waiting 12 minutes – no apology given.

Went through details of the dental questionnaire. Not sufficiently confidential, other patients could hear.

Fantastic greeting by dentist in the surgery. Completely wowed by before-and-after software, showing how appearance can be improved.

Very clear details provided on number and length of appointments, process and payment options.

Left practice an educated patient. Was telephoned twice afterwards to see if more information needed. However, never asked if wanted to go ahead with treatment. Too busy?

Details of the mystery shopper's physical visit are fed back for information and action.

Waiting times need to be analysed for existing patients to ensure great service. What is the acceptable waiting time for a new patient?

The telephone version gives data on prices, which are used as a basis for the new financial year. This is the time when new prices are set as well as revised laboratory fees and dental costs.

Although not used by many practices, the mystery shopper exercise is a key tool in your treatment plan conversion process.

When was the last time you carried out a mystery shopper on your own business? Action points arise from this.

A detailed mystery shopper report is provided at Appendix I (see page xxxi).

Get the Best for the Job

Add specific skills to your team

As stated previously, dentists generally don't like to sell and you may employ a Treatment Coordinator to handle treatment plan conversion.

If you do employ team members with specific skills, you have to consider how you use them to get the best results. Options include:

- the patient comes out of the surgery and goes into the Treatment Coordination room; here the Treatment Coordinator or a nurse explains the treatment, price and finance options available

- the patient receives treatment, gets a treatment plan for the future and leaves with no decision made

- conversion occurs while the patient is in the chair, agreeing to the treatment plan on the same visit.

The ideal situation is to obtain a decision as soon as possible rather than losing control of the process. Any delay requires follow-up telephone calls or further free booked consultations and lessens the chances of a positive outcome.

41 Role of the Reception Team

Treat as customers not patients

When in the surgery, people are patients, but in the reception area they are customers.

There is a difference and it's important to get the approach right.

When people come into the reception area, they must be made welcome. They need to be greeted and treated properly, as you would with hotel and restaurant guests. Consequently, members of the reception team must have good customer service skills.

Once people move into the surgery, they become patients and the approach is quite different. Since clinical work is being done, they expect quality and competence.

The difference is quite distinct and the systems and procedures must be adapted to reflect this.

Don't underestimate the value of the reception area as a sales environment.

Get testimonials from delighted patients/clients and put these up on the walls (also on the website, in brochures and any other literature).

The important thing is to have a consistent system to capture great words used by delighted patients and customers.

42 Sales Conversion

The importance of prompt and effective action

If you give a patient a treatment plan and let them walk out of the door without making a decision, you've lost control.

They can go elsewhere or do nothing.

Before they leave, offer a free consultation within the next two weeks. Ask them to bring a partner to discuss the treatment plan. In this way, you still have control unless they cancel.

The ideal situation, however, is the patient makes an immediate decision.

The whole treatment plan conversion process has to be measured, structured and followed up. By structuring the conversion process, you ensure training and systems are apparent at every stage. This covers the way:

- the telephone is answered
- patients are greeted
- patients are taken into the surgery and spoken to there
- patients are spoken to at the treatment plan conversion stage
- treatment plans are followed up
- patients are spoken to for the second time after their visit.

Treat every patient as an individual and approach them in a way that's appropriate for their character. For example:

- an analytical person needs to know the cost and detail of their treatment
- a creative person wants to see how he or she will look (use a before-and-after software tool to illustrate)
- a busy person simply wants to know how much and when.

Adapt your treatment plan conversion process to the style of the individual and you achieve the best results.

Team

Consider this ...

Do you employ staff or a team?

Are you part of the staff or part of a team?

Success is built on teamwork.

Foster a team, where your team members support, develop and inspire each other, and your practice will reach heights you didn't know it could reach.

Start to do this now and ban the word 'staff' in your practice. Insist everyone refers to 'team' instead from now on.

This section describes how you ensure you build a team in the true sense of the word and make sure everyone is fulfilling the correct role.

43 Get the Right Team to Ensure You Achieve Your Aims

It's not a new saying but it's nevertheless true: 'There's no "I" in team.'

In other words, it's not about individuals, it's about how everyone works together.

You need your team so you achieve your vision and mission. They have to understand the direction in which the practice is going so they fulfil their own career ambitions and are part of a great business.

Do you have the right team to achieve your vision and mission?

Jack Welch of GEC once said there are superstars, potential superstars and plodders, and you need a mix of all three for a successful team with underperformers out the door.

There are underperformers in every team and so, as the leader, you have to:

- identify training required and implement it
- measure the training results
- mentor each individual to achieve his or her potential.

If members of your team are still underperforming, responsibilities and accountabilities must be enforced. This enables the individuals to perform to their true potential, otherwise they're likely to leave the practice due to finding the process too demanding.

Profile your team to make sure you have the right people in their best roles. Identify any gaps and recruit appropriately.

44 Match Roles to Team Members

Ensure everyone knows what they have to do and can do it

Issue every individual with an organisation chart, their job title and job description so they know where they stand.

Particular information must be highlighted for each team member:

- their key tasks
- their key responsibilities
- key systems used
- key measurements
- key training required.

Performance can be measured daily, weekly, monthly or annually. This depends on the individual and their position within the practice.

When you identify a gap for a new role within the team, adopt a key interviewing process when filling the position. Go back to the profiling technique (see Chapter 12) and aim to match each candidate with the job description.

If you're taking on a new clinical person (such as a dentist or hygienist), it's absolutely imperative you pay for the person to come in for a day before making the appointment. This takes the form of a paid trial where the candidate will actually treat patients.

As Principal, you should observe the trial and assess the person's:

- social skills
- technical skills
- ability to communicate with the patient

- treatment plan conversion skills

- method of closing the appointment.

Undertake this type of assessment for all your dentists, hygienists and dental therapists. The purpose is to see how they measure up to the calibre and skills of the professionals currently working in the practice.

Ensure everyone starts on a six-month trial basis and this situation is clear to them at the commencement of their employment. It's also important you get all relevant employment advice regarding contracts.

Sir John Harvey-Jones said if he didn't see a light in the front-line people's eyes, he knew there was something missing in their direction.

If you use the right language in job advertisements or on recruitment websites, you are more likely to attract the right kind of individuals to the practice.

In addition to their technical and other skills, you want each member to buy in fully and be able to explain to every individual the vision, mission and core values of the practice.

45 Appraise Team Members to Ensure They Achieve Their Potential

The aim of appraisals is to set objectives for those being appraised and to ensure those objectives are achieved.

For clinicians, some of this can be dealt with on a regular monthly basis in team meetings. Quality, service and treatment plans can be assessed to ensure their performance is meeting patients' needs.

For most team members, the appraisal process occurs every three, six or twelve months. It assesses the objectives achieved during the previous period and those to be achieved in the future up to the next appraisal. Regular feedback is also given to improve performance.

If appraisals are held twice a year and the practice has a March year-end, appraisals are conducted in February and set objectives to be achieved by September. These are reviewed at the second appraisal, around October, and pay rises are agreed by March for the new financial year.

Actual frequencies are determined by the Principal, who may be involved in every appraisal. Individuals attending each appraisal will depend on who is being appraised. For example:

- Practice Manager/Business Manager and Head Receptionist for the reception team

- Practice Manager/Business Manager and Head Nurse for the nursing team

- Principal and Practice Manager/Business Manager for the Head Receptionist, Head Nurse or Clinician

- Principal and independent person conduct the Practice Manager/Business Manager appraisals.

Always ensure more than one person conducts appraisals so they are effective and legal. An independent person may be any trusted individual (such as an accountant or solicitor).

If required, coaching is available for Practice Managers, Business Managers and Principals so they conduct appraisals effectively and maximise the efficiency of the process.

Any forms used in the appraisal process need to be informative and relevant. They must be sent to the appraisee at least two days before the appraisal takes place. Appendix J has a sample appraisal form and a career development review form (see pages xxxii and xxxiii).

Allow sufficient time to complete each appraisal and ensure notes are taken for each session. These must be typed up and signed by both parties as a record of the appraisal.

The notes are placed on the appraisee's personal file with key objectives highlighted and the date they have to be achieved marked. All objectives need to be based on SMART principles (see Chapter 4) to ensure the appraisal process is effective.

Information Technology

Information technology (IT) is a key element of any business nowadays and it's no different for a dental practice.

Having the right IT hardware and software in place enables your practice to operate efficiently. The data you need is quickly available and you are able to see the progress you are making.

Don't underestimate the importance of good IT systems as an integral part of your operation.

46 Application Software

Provide the information for your practice needs

Effective IT is about getting the information you need, when you need it.

It's very rare a practice is so specialised it needs custom software. You can generally find package applications to meet your needs.

There are a number of basic applications to install to meet the requirements of your practice. If you don't feel confident to choose the software that's right for you, get help from an IT specialist to avoid making mistakes.

You need a mixture of general business software and some that's specifically designed for dentists. Essential applications are:

Email to handle your messages. Whatever you choose, ensure:

- sensitive details are kept confidential and secure; encrypt messages to prevent unauthorised access

- outgoing messages go to the correct people; check the address before sending

- received messages are responded to promptly, especially enquiries from the website.

Financial for your accounting and forecasting needs. Popular packages with the required features are Sage, QuickBooks, Quicken and VT Transaction. Whichever you choose, make sure users get the necessary training and can maximise the reporting functions of the software.

Marketing to handle your campaigns and record their effectiveness. Make sure you know the application's capability and how often it is updated.

Practice software designed specifically for dentists. Applications include Software of Excellence, R4, TAB Dental and Chiral.

Chiral is a relatively new application adapted specifically for individual dental needs. This includes the provision of KPIs to achieve your vision and mission, and the ability to produce customised reports.

There are several different practice applications on the market. You need to find one that is appropriate for your practice and provides the required reporting.

Many practice applications incorporate the functionality of other software that otherwise has to be bought separately (financial, marketing, paperless office). This avoids the need to integrate data from different applications.

For any practice software, training is imperative so users are familiar with the application's functionality. Ideally, training is staged so your team understands the relevant aspects of the software. Trying to learn everything at once usually means some of it is forgotten.

The practice software you choose must provide the ability to record the following key information for each patient as a minimum (in addition to all clinical details):

- contact and other relevant details
- how they prefer to be recalled (letter, telephone, email, text)
- their profession (for marketing opportunities)
- referral or marketing source (how referred or by whom)
- religion
- category of patient (gold, NHS*, etc. see Chapter 30)
- family members (whether patients or not)
- recall frequency (for examinations or hygienist visits)
- specific notes regarding the individual (e.g. enjoys golf, moved house, new baby, date given referral cards so you don't repeat too early).

Once these records are set up, identify any gaps. Task your reception team members with obtaining the missing information and enter it into the file. It's particularly important that recall frequencies and dates are recorded so patients aren't forgotten.

47 Get the Right Hardware

Ensure it fits your needs and is secure

IT hardware is a specialist area.

If you don't fully understand what's required, get relevant advice from an IT specialist. It costs you money but pays dividends in the long term if you get the correct equipment and use it properly.

Fail to get proper advice and you are in danger of being mis-sold what you need for your practice.

You require equipment with enough speed and capacity to handle your requirements, not only now but for some time into the future.

You don't want the cost and disruption of having to change equipment soon after you buy it because it's not up to the job. At the same time, don't buy something that's far too powerful for your needs because that's an unnecessary expense.

A qualified and experienced IT specialist is able to specify equipment to do the job based on your business needs. If the practice is growing fast and is largely paperless, for example, you may require a bigger server than you originally thought.

Apart from processing speed and storage capacity, the hardware has to be able to run the different software you are to use. It must support integration between the various applications.

Don't forget, hardware does sometimes break down. Ensure you have the appropriate support contracts for your business needs.

The extent of the support and the response times must be adequate so the practice doesn't suffer because the IT equipment is out of action. On the other hand, don't buy support that is more than you need. Having a 24/7 support contract might be essential for an online shopping operation but is over the top for a dental practice.

Be very clear about what's covered and what isn't. Finding out you don't have the necessary cover when you need it can come as a nasty shock.

> Stay safe

What you must also do is ensure everything is safe, secure and in order. This means you:

- have adequate physical security measures, with servers in locked rooms

- prevent unauthorised access by having proper password protection on all PCs, ensure unattended machines are logged off and other measures are taken

- have full Internet protection, including firewalls and anti-virus software, to prevent data being stolen or corrupted

- introduce regular back-up procedures, with data copies stored off-site or at least in a fireproof safe

- check your back-up copies to ensure you can restore from them if necessary

- maintain an asset register of all equipment and security mark most items

- have the appropriate licences for everything you run

- ensure you adhere to the provisions of the Data Protection Act.

As well as breaking down, equipment does become worn out, is superseded or outdated. Make sure, therefore, you have a proper replacement policy and your annual forecast (see Chapter 28) has provision for the cost of new hardware.

Clinical

It's your dental practice so I have no intention of telling you how to run your own clinical systems.

However, there are certain key areas to focus on.

This section covers why you look at your patient numbers and the types of work you provide.

It also deals with how you maximise your hygiene potential, improve your recall rates and keep your clinical systems up to date.

48 Know Who You're Dealing With

Get an accurate patient list

You may know how many patients you have on your records but how many of them are active?

Checking your patient records can lead to a nasty shock. A lot of them may not be active and may no longer be patients at all.

Go through your patient records periodically to see which ones are active. At least you clear out the dead wood and end up with a representative patient list. You also know if you need to step up your marketing and sales efforts to increase your patient numbers.

Firstly, establish how many patients you have. Then go through the list and identify those who haven't attended the practice for 18 months or more. You need to determine if these people are still active patients.

Create a regular follow-up system where you communicate with and educate those who haven't been attending. Speak with each one or ask them to contact the practice.

Find out if they still consider themselves to be patients. If not, archive their records or, if they have moved to another dentist, pass on their details.

Keeping your patient list up to date and correct is the responsibility of your Practice Manager, assisted by the reception team. This task is particularly important if you think of selling the practice because an accurate patient list is essential for the contract.

49 Know Your Services

And ensure each type of work is properly resourced

To market and run your practice properly, you have to know what's on offer.

Identify all your services and list them. These may include:

- dental examinations
- hygiene
- fillings
- crowns and bridges
- dentures
- implants
- veneers
- periodontal
- endodontics
- orthodontics
- oral surgery
- sedation
- mouth guards
- maxillofacial surgery
- apicectomy
- Botox/derma fillers.

Make all necessary educational material available for every service to ensure your marketing and treatment plan conversion is effective. You also have to ensure all relevant education material, systems and instruments are not only available but also conform to the British Dental Association Good Practice Scheme and Care Quality Commission procedures.

50 Maximise Your Hygiene Potential and Increase Your Revenue

Patients who don't see the hygienist are a potential source of additional revenue.

Consider the following example:

> Number of active private patients = 1,000
>
> 90% of them should see the hygienist = 900 (this ignores children who cannot use the service)
>
> Number of active patients seeing hygienist = 450
>
> Potential patients to see hygienist = 450
>
> Therefore:
>
> 2 visits @ 30 minutes per year = £110 income/£75 profit per hour
>
> Potential profit is 450 patients x £75 = £33,750 per annum.

Introduce a system to achieve full hygiene potential. For instance:

- print a full patient list with details of services used
- highlight those who do not see hygienists
- make dentists aware they must refer patients to hygienists
- encourage the use of dental mirrors and cameras to help the process by letting patients see the problem
- produce reports on each dentist to measure patients referred and not converted.

All dentists must ensure patients are fit for hygiene treatment. The converse of this is some patients are at risk if they don't see the hygienist – bad oral hygiene can result in bacteria entering the blood stream, which can cause heart problems.

Treat the hygiene function of the practice with great respect. Chances are it has great potential for growth.

51 Examinations and Hygiene Recalls

Get the system right to increase patient visits

Examinations are the engine room of your practice since they generate work in all sorts of areas.

Assess your patient numbers to see the potential, for example:

- 1,200 active patients

- all should be seen once or twice a year (depending on protocols and policies), this gives 1,200–2,400 potential visits

- half see the hygienist between one and four times a year, so there is the potential for 600–2,400 hygienist sessions.

Compare your potential visits to actual visits achieved. Find out if there is a shortfall you need to address.

If the numbers don't work out, there may be some deficiencies in your recall procedure you need to correct. Have a look at your recall rates:

> 1,200 patients seen twice a year.
>
> 200 recall letters a month (or a mix of recall letters and pre-booked appointments).
>
> Always send recall letters at the start of the previous month (if appointment is due March, letter goes out early February).
>
> If 200 letters are sent and 150 are booked in by the end of the following month, the recall rate is 75%.
>
> A 50% rate means 100 patients are either not coming in or slipping to the following month.

Measurements are key to check if your recall system is effective. These measurements are part of the One Page™ Plan (see Chapter 16). Poor recall rates affect all areas of your practice – marketing, revenue and cash flow.

If your recall rates are poor, how do you improve them?

First, look at your system to see if you are contacting patients in the way they have requested (letter, telephone, etc.) and at the right frequency. If most contact is by letter, have a look at what you send to see if it can be improved. Most practice software can produce template letters you can use.

> Effective recall letters

Consider the following:

> Dear X,
>
> Your dental examination is now due. Please contact the surgery to arrange an appointment.
>
> Yours sincerely,
> Y

This is neither exciting nor likely to motivate patients to take action.

Your recall letter is important for marketing purposes and so has to be effective. The following example is much better:

> Dear X,
>
> Your dental examination is now due.
>
> During the examination, we check for early signs of dental problems, such as decay or gum disease, and take measures to prevent the problems from becoming serious. This could save a lot of pain, time and money.
>
> Please contact the surgery. If we have not heard from you within seven working days, we will contact you to arrange an appointment.
>
> Yours faithfully,
> Y

This second example is much better in two ways:

- It shows the value of the dental examination (the same can apply for hygiene recall letters).

- Control is not lost because someone will follow up if the patient makes no contact. Systemise this contact and make sure a team member is accountable for the process.

This type of letter has more chance of generating high recall rates.

You may also offer promotions ('25 per cent off whitening') and can include referral cards (see Chapter 33).

If recall rates are low (such as 40 per cent or below), offer patients the opportunity to join a plan (Practice Plan or DPAS, for example).

In these cases, the patient pays a set amount each year and the plan provides for a number of examinations and a percentage discount off treatment costs.

Plans are important to a practice. Their big advantage is they provide a constant flow of revenue even if the patients don't attend.

52 Systems

Update your clinical systems regularly to ensure they meet the needs of your practice.

Your systems should adhere to the format described in Chapter 19.

Apart from benefiting the practice, great systems win you awards. These include British Dental Association awards, Investors in People and other dentistry awards.

Systems are at the heart of quality and clinical governance. Responsibilities set through these systems must be apparent to all members of the team.

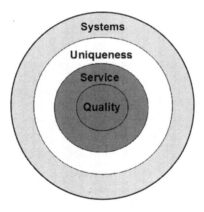

Endgame

You now have your hands on what you need to turn your practice into a dental business. What you do with the information is up to you. Apply these principles and you will create a dental practice that will give you:

- a capital value to enjoy your retirement or

- a great feeling of being able to pass on a successful business to your family or

- the ability to remain an owner or shareholder of a successful practice.

Whatever endgame you choose, if you adhere to this advice, you will achieve your goals and have a successful business life.

Valuers of dental businesses are increasingly using more sophisticated methods of valuation. They will look at:

- revenue

- profit known as EBITDA – earnings before interest, tax, depreciation and amortisation

- new patients and their type

- reputation

- systems within the practice

- the management team

- the Principal's clinical work on a monthly basis.

The right valuer will maximise the sale price of your practice. You need to find one who will deal with your endgame expectations.

I wish you great success in all you achieve on your vision, mission, personal and business goals, as you continue to uphold your core values.
Enjoy the journey!

I hope you have benefitted from this book. A great first step to take now is to log on to the Clear Vision Dental website: www.clearvisiondental.co.uk and complete the checklist which measures your business on the 5 key factors proven to give dentists greater results and bigger rewards. Complete this and you will discover where your practice is strong and the areas where it can improve. Plus you will ABSOLUTELY, DEFINITELY know where to start to improve your results and increase the rewards you see from your practice.

Appendix A
How to create the perfect mission statement

Most corporate mission statements are worthless because they consist largely of pious platitudes such as: 'We will hold ourselves to the highest standards of professionalism and ethical behaviour.'

Others are worthless because they state necessities as if they were objectives. For example, 'to achieve sufficient profit' – which is the same as a person saying their mission is to breathe sufficiently. It may be a necessity ... but it will hardly inspire you on to greatness!

Another example of a worthless mission statement came from a multinational chemical firm, whose main products were cyanide derivatives. They insisted that the same mission statement be used in every one of their subsidiary businesses throughout the world. And that global mission statement read something like: 'We aim not to kill more than 100 people this year through cyanide poisoning'!!! Obviously, while only killing 100 people may have been seen as a worthwhile target, it was a PR disaster!

> The keys to writing a great mission statement

A mission statement should not merely commit the business to what it must do to survive.

Instead, it should commit the business to what it has chosen to do in order to thrive.

And it should not be filled with operationally meaningless superlatives such as 'biggest', 'best', 'optimum' and 'maximum'. For example, one company says it wants to 'maximise its growth potential', another 'to provide products of the highest quality'. But how can either company determine whether it is actually achieving its maximum growth potential or the highest quality?

Nothing should be included in a mission statement if it cannot be disagreed with reasonably. For example, can you imagine any company disagreeing with the objective 'to provide the best value for the money'? If you can't, it's not worth saying in your mission statement!

> What other characteristics should a great mission statement have?

1. it should explain the company's objectives in a way that enables progress towards those objectives to be measured. To state objectives that cannot be used to evaluate performance is hypocrisy.

Unless the mission statement changes the behaviour of the firm that makes it, it has no value. For example, the behaviour of a Mexican firm was profoundly affected by the following passage from its mission statement:

> " To create a wholesome, varied, pluralistic, multiclass recreational area incorporating tourist facilities and permanent residences, and to produce locally as much of the goods and services required by the area as possible, so as to improve the standard of living and quality of life of its inhabitants. "

2. a company's mission statement should differentiate it from other companies. It should establish the individuality, if not the uniqueness, of the firm.

A company that wants only what most other companies want – for example, 'to manufacture products in an efficient manner, at costs that help yield adequate profits' – wastes its time in formulating a mission statement.

3. a mission statement should define the business that the company wants to be in, not necessarily the business that it is in already. After all, having a mission is about creating a better future – not simply taking stock of the past and present.

However diverse its current business, the company should try to find a unifying concept that enlarges its view of itself and brings it into focus.

For example, a company that produces beverages, snacks and baked goods and operates a variety of dining, recreational and entertainment facilities identified its business as 'increasing the satisfaction people derive from use of their free time'. This suggested completely new directions for its diversification and growth.

4. a mission statement should be relevant to all the firm's stakeholders. These include its customers, suppliers, the public, shareholders and employees.

The mission should state how the company intends to serve each of these stakeholders.

For example, one company committed itself to providing all its employees with 'adequate and fair compensation, safe working conditions, stable employment, challenging work, opportunities for personal development and a satisfying quality of work life'. It also wanted 'to provide those who supply the material used in the business with continuing, if not expanding, sources of business and with incentives to improve their products and services and their use through research and development'.

Most mission statements address only shareholders and managers. Their most serious deficiency is their failure to motivate non-managerial employees. Without their commitment, a company's mission has little chance of being fulfilled ... whatever its managers and shareholders do.

5. and of greatest importance, a mission statement should be exciting and inspiring. It should motivate everyone who is going to be involved in making the mission come true – and that will often mean everybody.

For example, one Latin American company committed itself to being 'an active force for economic and social development, fostering economic integration of Latin America and, within each country, collaboration between government, industry, labour and the public'.

A mission should play the same role in a company that the Holy Grail did in the Crusades. It does not have to appear to be feasible; it only has to be desirable.

> ... man has been able to grow enthusiastic over his vision of ... unconvincing enterprises. He has put himself to work for the sake of an idea, seeking by magnificent exertions to arrive at the incredible. And in the end he has arrived there. Beyond all doubt it is one of the vital sources of man's power, to be thus able to kindle enthusiasm from the mere glimmer of something improbable, difficult, remote.

One final tip ... keep it simple and short. Many practices make the mistake of going on for pages and pages – and as a result bore their readers rigid! It is far better to make it crisp and punchy. Use simple language. And, if there is a lot to say, use bullet points to make it easier to read and digest.

> Using the right language

Choosing the correct words is of critical importance. So to help you, here is a list of words/short phrases that tend to work well:

- **Adverbs** – assertively, authoritatively, collaboratively, competently, completely, continually, conveniently, dramatically, efficiently, enthusiastically, globally, interactively, quickly, proactively, professionally, seamlessly, synergistically

- **Verbs** – administrate, build, coordinate, create, customise, disseminate, engineer, enhance, facilitate, fashion, foster, initiate, integrate, leverage existing, leverage other's, maintain, negotiate, network, promote, provide access to, pursue, restore, revolutionise, simplify, supply, utilise

- **Adjectives** – competitive, corporate, cost-effective, cutting-edge, diverse, economically sound, effective, emerging, error-free, ethical, enterprise-wide, excellent, high-payoff, high-quality, high standards in, inexpensive, innovative, interdependent, long-term high-impact, low-risk high-yield, market-driven, mission-critical, parallel, performance-based, professional, progressive, prospective, quality, scaleable, timely, unique, value-added, virtual, world-class

- **Nouns** – business, benefits, catalysts for change, content, data, deliverables, information, infrastructures, intellectual capital, leadership skills, materials, methods of empowerment, opportunities, paradigms, products, resources, services, solutions, sources, technology

> Mission statement checklist

A mission statement checklist follows, summarising everything covered in these notes.

Please use it to help you write a mission statement that motivates and enthuses everybody involved in your business so that they help you drive your business on to ever-greater heights.

	Issues to consider	Notes
1	Does it commit your business to what you have chosen to do in order to thrive – instead of what you must do in order to survive?	
2	Could a reasonable person disagree with everything in your mission statement?	
3	Are the things in your mission statement measurable?	
4	Is it likely to cause your business and its people to do things differently and/or do different things?	
5	Does it differentiate you from everyone else?	
6	Does it clearly define what you want to be – instead of just stating what you already are?	
7	Is it relevant to all stakeholders, including: • Patients • Suppliers • Shareholders • Your team • Society	
8	Does it talk to all team members – and is it likely to motivate and enthuse them?	
9	Is it exciting and inspiring?	
10	Is it crisp, simple and short?	
11	If it is more than a few sentences long, does it use a bullet-point style to make it easier to read and digest?	
12	Does it use the right kind of language?	

> *Important notes*

- Please look very carefully at any areas where you have answered 'No', since there is a very real risk that they will prevent your mission statement (and your practice) from being as successful as it could be.

- This checklist should be read in conjunction with the rest of Appendix A, since it explains what each point means and why they are so important.

B

Appendix B

Patient journeys compared

You move to a new area and want to choose a new dentist – which practice would you use – X or Y?

Dental practice X	Dental practice Y
Phone answered in seven rings	Two rings
Gruff voice	Friendly voice
Person you need is away from desk, but they promise to ring you back – it takes two hours	Rings you back in two minutes
Before the appointment they send you a map showing you how to find them	As well as sending you the map, they ring you up to check that you received the map, tell you where to park and check that you know where to come
Reception table is covered in magazines and newspapers – which are out of date	Only thing open on the table is a beautifully bound volume containing press cuttings and testimonial letter
The phone rings seven times when you have a query to be answered and then goes to answerphone	Phone answered at all times
Team uses technical language and jargon	Team explains that it is a jargon-free zone and proceeds to only use plain English
The dentist lists the options but doesn't actually come off the fence and give you a clear recommendation	The dentist comes off the fence and says 'If it were me I would…'
The dentist only answers the questions you ask	The dentist probes to make sure that he identifies the real issues, not just restricting himself to the things you ask about

Dental practice X	Dental practice Y
Four days later you receive a letter by post, accompanied by a self-congratulatory glossy brochure	Four hours later a welcome letter arrives by email. There is no brochure, but the letter does come complete with a) scanned testimonial letters from patients they have done similar work for, b) service guarantees, c) a letter from the Principal saying how excited they all are about treating you
Price = ?	Price = ?

What price differential would you make?

C Appendix C

Your Team Day agenda

1. Review of agenda

2. The business model

3. Agree the vision and mission for the business

4. Review of practice business goals

5. Measurements to achieve the vision and mission

6. Five things that you would change or improve in the practice

7. Review of Principal's reverse appraisal

8. The value of systems

9. Ideal patient/patient categorisation

10. Project plan with deadlines

Appendix D
Measurement aids

> *SWOT worksheet*

Strengths	Weaknesses
What makes people use the practice?	What skills do we lack and what aren't we good at?
Who recommends us?	What do others do better than us?
What makes patients recommend us?	What failures have we had recently and why?
What skills do we have and what are we especially good at?	Why do people choose our competitors instead of us?
What can we do that nobody else can?	
What successes have we had recently and why?	Why do previously happy patients leave us?

Opportunities	Threats
What new products/services could we offer?	What new ideas, techniques and technology could undermine us?
What new skills and capabilities could we acquire?	What are our competitors doing that could damage us?
How could we become unique?	Are there any legal, economic, social or political threats to us?
What new types of patients/markets/needs could we serve?	Are our patients' needs changing?
What changes in the market could we exploit?	What other changes in the market could damage us?
What new ideas, techniques and technology could we use?	Are there any other black clouds on the horizon?

> Small business success

Measure your practice against the top 10 reasons why small businesses fail, according to Michael Gerber.

1. **Lack of management systems.** Systems are the key to creating a business that works ... without you having to be there. This in turn will allow you to work 'on' the business, increase the value of your business, ensure your customers get a consistent level of service and motivate your people.

   On a scale of 1 to 10 (where 1 is very poor and 10 is excellent), how comprehensive are the systems in your business?

   Please circle

   1   2   3   4   5   6   7   8   9   10

2. **Lack of vision and purpose by principals.** *'Where is the business heading?'*

   On a scale of 1 to 10 (where 1 is very poor and 10 is excellent), how clear are your written goals?

   Please circle

   1   2   3   4   5   6   7   8   9   10

3. **Lack of financial planning and review.** It is essential to have access to regular management information and hold regular board meetings.

   On a scale of 1 to 10 (where 1 is very poor and 10 is excellent), how accurate and regular is your management information?

   Please circle

   1   2   3   4   5   6   7   8   9   10

4. **Overdependence on specific individuals in the business.** Develop your business around 'functions' not 'people'. If specific individuals are vital to your business, ensure that you have key person insurance in place.

On a scale of 1 to 10 (where 1 is very poor and 10 is excellent), how well will the business fare if key individuals (including yourself) leave or become unable to work?

Please circle

1   2   3   4   5   6   7   8   9   10

5. **Poor market segmentation and strategy.** Do you know who you want to market to (type of customer) and how you want to portray your business in the marketplace (e.g. the cheapest or a premium product/service)?

On a scale of 1 to 10 (where 1 is very poor and 10 is excellent), how clearly defined is your ideal patient and the positioning of your business in the marketplace?

Please circle

1   2   3   4   5   6   7   8   9   10

6. **Lack of knowledge about the market and competition.** Do you undertake market research and competitor analysis? For example, chocolates used to be a popular gift but they are now being replaced by wine, flowers and gift vouchers.

On a scale of 1 to 10 (where 1 is very poor and 10 is excellent), how good is your knowledge of your competitors and your marketplace?

Please circle

1   2   3   4   5   6   7   8   9   10

7. **Failure to establish or communicate company goals.**
Communication is one of the keys to motivating your people.

On a scale of 1 to 10 (where 1 is very poor and 10 is excellent), how comprehensive are your communication systems in your business?

Please circle

1   2   3   4   5   6   7   8   9   10

8. **Absence of a standardised quality programme.**

On a scale of 1 to 10 (where 1 is very poor and 10 is excellent), how comprehensive are your systems to ensure quality in your business?

Please circle

1   2   3   4   5   6   7   8   9   10

9. **Inadequate capitalisation or lack of funds.** Cash flow is all-important for a business. Many profitable businesses fail due to lack of cash.

On a scale of 1 to 10 (where 1 is very poor and 10 is excellent), how secure is your cash flow position?

Please circle

1   2   3   4   5   6   7   8   9   10

10. **Owners concentrating on the technical, rather than strategic, work at hand.** Are you running a business or are you self-employed?

On a scale of 1 to 10 (where 1 is very poor and 10 is excellent), how well are you using your time to work on your business?

Please circle

1   2   3   4   5   6   7   8   9   10

There are three parts of business development:

- **Innovation.** By recognising that it is not the *commodity* that demands innovation but the process by which it is sold, the franchisor aims his/her innovative energies at the way in which his/her business does business. *You will only ever come up with the innovations when you work on your business.*

- **Quantification.** Without it, how would you know that the innovation worked? Remember, *what you can measure you can manage.* You must measure everything that you do.

- **Orchestration.** The elimination of discretion or choice at the operating level of your business. *You need a system ...*

According to Michael Gerber, there are four systems:

- How we do it here – differentiation from everybody else

- How we recruit, hire and train people to do it here

- How we manage here – management system

- How we change it here – this is never-ending ... things must continually change.

Are all of these in your 'systems manual'?

> *KickStart questionnaire*

Measure these personal and business areas and you start to highlight the strengths you have to use and the weaknesses you need to address:

Business: ....

Completed by: .... Date: ....

1.	On a scale of 0–100 (where 0 = terrible, 50 = average, 100 = outstanding), how good:

Are your time management skills? ....

Are your leadership skills? ....

Are your delegation skills? ....

Are your communication skills? ....

2.	How happy does your business make you? To answer this question put a *cross* at the appropriate point on the line below.

Very stressed. Very unhappy. I work far too hard. It doesn't pay anywhere near well enough. I feel trapped.

About the same as everyone else. The business has its good and bad moments. I work harder and get rewarded less than I would like. There is some stress.

I love it and couldn't be happier. It pays really well and I really look forward to coming to work.

3. On a scale of 0–100 (where 0 = terrible, 50 = average, 100 = outstanding), how good is your business at:

Marketing – i.e. creating sales leads? ....

Sales – i.e. converting leads into sales? ....

Charging what you are really worth? ....

Operations – i.e. making and providing whatever it is that you sell? ....

Customer service – i.e. keeping customers happy? ....

After-sales care? ....

Handling complaints? ....

Getting paid what you are owed? ....

Producing reliable products and services? ....

Motivating its people? ....

Training its people? ....

Getting the best from its people? ....

Generating new ideas? ....

Putting new ideas into practice? ....

Launching new products? ....

Making the most of leading-edge technologies? ....

Controlling costs? ....

Measuring exactly how well it is doing at all times? ....

4. Read the description of the three businesses below and put a *cross* on the line to signify where your business is in comparison to them.

This business has no systems at all. The business owner has to drive everything. And as a result he works 60 hours a week sorting out problems, covering for absent team members, fighting fires and making things happen. He never seems to have time for things like planning since he is always busy working on more urgent things. And he only manages to take two weeks' holiday a year – when he spends the whole time worrying about how everyone will be coping without him!

This business has the same basic systems as everyone else in the industry. But, like the rest of the industry, most of what it does is not systemised. And if key people aren't around, some things don't get done well (and sometimes they don't get done at all!). As a result, the business owner works 47.5 hours a week (which research shows is exactly average for the owner of a UK small business). And, by working hard like that every week, he just about manages to take four weeks' holiday a year. In other words, it is a typical and very average small business.

This business has systems for everything – containing everything everybody needs to know to run the business effectively and profitably. They are also continuously tested and improved, and everybody knows exactly what they are and how they work – so everybody uses them. As a result the business owner usually works only 35 hours a week and took six weeks off as holiday last year (when he didn't worry once about the business because he knew it would work perfectly without him).

5. Now put a *star* on the line to show where you would like your business to be. *Remember, the cross you have already put on the line shows where you believe your business is now.*

> *Reverse appraisal form*

Please tell us what you think.

[name of dental business]

We are carrying out this team survey to give you a chance to express your views about what the business does well – and where and how it could do even better. So it is obviously important that you answer this survey as honestly as possible. Remember, there are no right or wrong answers; this exercise is purely to help improve our company and increase your job satisfaction.

And, of course, if there isn't enough room for your answers in the spaces given, please feel free to add extra sheets. After all, the more you tell us, the more we have to work on!

Although we want to be as open as possible, we also recognise that at this stage there may be some things you would rather say on a confidential basis. So, in return for your openness and participation, we guarantee the complete confidentiality of your answers.

You can be sure of confidentiality. Simply leave your completed questionnaire sealed in the tray provided and we will send it off, sealed as you leave it, to Clear Vision in one envelope with all the other forms from everyone. Clear Vision will then produce a summary report that contains no names. That summary report is all they will show to us. Clear Vision will also destroy all the original questionnaires and guarantee not to discuss any facts relating to any individual. Leave your name off the questionnaire if you want!

We are committed to responding to the issues you raise and the results will be published for all the team to see. In the meantime, thank you for taking part in this team survey and for contributing to the continuing success of our business.

[*partner/PM name here*]

RATING SCALE

1 = NEVER   2 = SELDOM   3 = USUALLY   4 = ALWAYS

A.	Has a positive attitude	
B.	Listens to employee concerns	
C.	Is available when others need him/her	
D.	Pulls his/her fair share of the workload	
E.	Is receptive to concerns about his/her performance	
F.	Supports improvement efforts in the department	
G.	Accepts accountability for own actions	
H.	Encourages an enjoyable work environment	
I.	Supports the team in professional development	
J.	Is receptive to patient needs	
K.	Asks the team for suggestions on improvement	
L.	Holds the team accountable for performance	
M.	Communicates the overall vision to the team	
N.	Communicates goals and initiatives to the team	
O.	Communicates goals and priorities specific to employee	
P.	Provides leadership to develop the team's vision and mission	
Q.	Encourages the team to participate in planning activities	
R.	Provides helpful direction on tasks	
S.	Allows for employee freedom as appropriate	
T.	Clearly communicates performance expectations	
U.	Resolves employee conflicts in an appropriate manner	
V.	Creates and supports a diverse working environment	

What actions would you like [*name*] to 'start' that he/she is not doing currently?

What actions would you prefer [*name*] to stop?

What suggestions or feedback would you offer for [*name*]'s improvement?

> Example of reverse appraisal review

Reverse appraisal of XYZ   Sept xx

Number of forms received: 5

1 = NEVER, 2 = SELDOM, 3 = USUALLY, 4 = ALWAYS

	Statement	1	2	3	4	5	Average	Trend
A.	Has a positive attitude	3	4	4	3	3	3.40	😊
B.	Listens to employee concerns	3	4	3	2	2.5	2.90	😐
C.	Is available when others need him/her	2	3	3	2	1.5	2.30	🙁
D.	Pulls his/her fair share of the workload	4	4	4	3	3	3.60	😊
E.	Is receptive to concerns about his/her performance	2	3	4	4	3	3.20	😊
F.	Supports improvement efforts in the department	4	4	4	4	4	4.00	😊
G.	Accepts accountability for own actions	2	3	4	3	2	2.80	😐
H.	Encourages an enjoyable work environment	3	4	4	4	3	3.60	😊
I.	Supports the team in professional development	3	4	4	4	3	3.60	😊
J.	Is receptive to patient needs	3	4	4	4	3	3.60	😊
K.	Asks the team for suggestions on improvement	3	4	3	3	3	3.20	😊
L.	Holds the team accountable for performance	3	3	3	4	3	3.20	😊
M.	Communicates the overall vision to the team	4	4	4	4	4	4.00	😊
N.	Communicates goals and initiatives to the team	3	4	4	3	4	3.60	😊
O.	Communicates goals and priorities specific to employee	3	4	4	3	4	3.60	😊
P.	Provides leadership to develop the team's vision and mission	2	3	3	4	1.5	2.70	😐
Q.	Encourages the team to participate in planning activities	3	4	3	3	4	3.40	😊
R.	Provides helpful direction on tasks	2	3	3	4	3.5	3.10	😊
S.	Allows for employee freedom as appropriate	3	4	3	3	3	3.20	😊
T.	Clearly communicates performance expectations	3	4	3	3	4	3.40	😊
U.	Resolves employee conflicts in an appropriate manner	1	2	3	2	1	1.80	😊
V.	Creates and supports a diverse working environment	3	3	3	3	2	2.80	😐

Appendix E

Practice Manager job description

The purpose of this role is to manage the surgery, reception and support team.

Principal duties and responsibilities

Financial

- Day-to-day reconciliations

- To assist in achieving turnover targets

- To ensure UDAs are being achieved

- To achieve all measurements as agreed on the One Page™ Plan, including the recall rate and hygiene growth

Marketing

- To ensure all new patient information is logged on Software of Excellence (SOE), including referral source

- To work on agreed strategic marketing plan

HR

- To maintain all employment procedures

- Team appraisals

- Daily management of team and keep team accountable to the actions and tasks they have agreed to undertake

Reception

- To ensure efficient operation of all reception systems

- To ensure SOE is managed effectively

- To maintain adequate staffing of reception at all times

Sales

- To ensure training and role play is given to all dentists regarding scoring and imagery to ensure treatment conversion growth is achieved

Clinical

- To ensure all systems are consistent and efficient across all surgeries

- To ensure all nurses and associates remain accountable for protocols and systems within the business

Project implementation

- To manage the business project plan and drive the projects in conjunction with project plan days

Facilities management

- Building and facility management

- Obtain and keep all licences and legally required paperwork up to date

Appendix F

Incorporation checklist

NAME ....

BUSINESS NAME ....

EMAIL ....

YOUR BUSINESS YEAR-END INCORPORATION CHECKLIST

	Valuer	Accountant or Clear Vision	YOU	Solicitor	IFA
Arrange a valuation of the business	✓	✓			
Discuss the transfer of the NHS contract (if applicable) prior to contacting the PCT			✓	✓	
Consider change of name and branding identity being a limited company – may be important from a valuation point of view			✓		
Set up new company at Companies House and select company year-end and registered office		✓	✓		
Agree level of share capital		✓	✓		
Agree issue of shares and directorships		✓	✓		
Discuss details of directors' duties		✓	✓		
Contact HM Revenue and Customs to advise of new company for Corporation Tax purposes (forms CT41g and 64-8)		✓			
Arrange transfer of VAT registration using forms VAT1 and VAT68 if appropriate		✓			
Discuss remuneration and dividend strategy. Discuss repayment of directors' loan account		✓			

	Valuer	Accountant or Clear Vision	YOU	Solicitor	IFA
Stop Class 2 National Insurance contributions and discuss impact of minimal NI on benefits and state pension		✓			
Check level of income required for pension purposes and advise financial adviser		✓			✓
Discuss whether company cars are relevant, amend vehicle registrations and notify HMRC as appropriate		✓			
Assess the relevant employment issues arising and obligations under the Transfer of Undertakings (Protection of Employment) Regulations 2006				✓	
Review employment contracts for any necessary changes			✓	✓	
Arrange issue of new PAYE scheme if appropriate – HMRC may just transfer existing scheme to limited company		✓			
Issue P45s and transfer employees to new scheme if necessary		✓			
Complete and submit P35 form if necessary		✓			
Arrange shareholders' agreement/directors' service contracts		✓	✓	✓	✓
Consider the property options open and the relevant consequences and tax implications		✓		✓	
Discuss landlord and rental agreements for property		✓	✓	✓	
Consider the preparation of the sale contract documentation, the breakdown of the price payable under the contract and its execution		✓		✓	✓
Review wills (should happen regularly)		✓	✓	✓	✓

	Valuer	Accountant or Clear Vision	YOU	Solicitor	IFA
Discuss potential stamp duty				✓	
Reprint stationery with new company name			✓		
Change insurance certificate – public liability, employer's liability, etc.			✓		
Check if consumer credit licence needs to be changed			✓		
Advise finance companies regarding any hire purchase agreements, leases, etc. All assets should be transferred to the company			✓		
Write to suppliers and patients informing them of the change and the (positive) reason		✓	✓		
Contact bank regarding transfer of account and any loans/overdrafts			✓		
Notify trade associations and inform any other regulatory bodies e.g. BDA			✓		
Transfer mobile telephone contracts into the new company name			✓		
Inform employees of proposed change		✓	✓		
Review Health and Safety notification requirement			✓		
Amend telephone book entry/ online entries			✓		
Computerised accounting records – check software licences and change over data to new period of account			✓		

Appendix G
Management accounts example

Chart of Accounts:

Page 1

	Actual	Ratio (%)	Budget	Variance
Sales				
Consultations	88,384.50	14.20	142,500.00	(54,115.50)
Crown and Bridge/Imp.	201,345.00	32.35	265,500.00	(64,155.00)
Dentures	2,320.00	0.37	12,000.00	(9,680.00)
Restorative	76,325.00	12.26	104,500.00	(28,175.00)
Misc.	6,450.70	1.04	11,500.00	(5,049.30)
Hygiene	86,053.00	13.83	128,000.00	(41,947.00)
Shop	3,883.18	0.62	5,500.00	(1,616.82)
Consultations	4,065.00	0.65	15,000.00	(10,935.00)
Periodontology	27,740.00	4.46	40,250.00	(12,510.00)
Crown, Bridgework & Dentures	5,900.00	0.95	18,700.00	(12,800.00)
Periodontal Regeneration	1,200.00	0.19	0.00	1,200.00
Implants - Surgery	20,950.00	3.37	37,500.00	(16,550.00)
Implants	21,170.00	3.40	41,600.00	(20,430.00)
Restorative	5,140.00	0.83	21,950.00	(16,810.00)
Misc.	352.25	0.06	0.00	352.25
SC	28,390.00	4.56	21,000.00	7,390.00
Consultations	10,343.00	1.66	32,500.00	(22,157.00)
Crown & Bridgework	7,325.00	1.18	27,850.00	(20,525.00)
Restorative	16,355.00	2.63	36,600.00	(20,245.00)
Misc.	8,510.00	1.37	7,550.00	960.00
Seminar Income	126.00	0.02	0.00	126.00
	622,327.63	100.00	970,000.00	(347,672.37)
Purchases				
Materials	8,911.96	1.43	5,950.00	2,961.96
Technical Fees	42,071.19	6.76	66,375.00	(24,303.81)
Technical Fees	2,486.00	0.40	4,640.00	(2,154.00)
Implant Comp.	4,963.18	0.80	6,000.00	(1,036.82)
Implant Comp.	7,091.42	1.14	0.00	7,091.42
Implant Comp.	244.91	0.04	0.00	244.91
Technical Fees	1,729.68	0.28	7,090.00	(5,360.32)
Materials	2,776.03	0.45	1,750.00	1,026.03
Hygiene Materials	329.91	0.05	2,400.00	(2,070.09)
Materials	6,657.33	1.07	5,730.00	927.33
Shop	4,160.66	0.67	2,400.00	1,760.66
Misc.	22.21	0.00	0.00	22.21
Shop (Adjustment)	(705.59)	(0.11)	0.00	(705.59)
	80,738.89	12.97	102,335.00	(21,596.11)
Direct Expenses				
Hygiene Prof. Services	31,387.11	5.04	47,360.00	(15,972.89)
Associate	20,213.16	3.25	48,710.00	(28,496.84)
Associate	38,215.30	6.14	85,195.00	(46,979.70)
Dent. Equip. Repairs & Service	6,850.26	1.10	2,850.00	4,000.26
Associate	14,150.00	2.27	0.00	14,150.00
Misc. Expenses	2,144.00	0.34	2,400.00	(256.00)
Seminar Costs	5,832.63	0.94	0.00	5,832.63
	118,792.46	19.09	186,515.00	(67,722.54)
Gross Profit/(Loss):	422,796.28	67.94	681,150.00	(258,353.72)
Overheads				
Gross Salaries	103,284.34	16.60	155,400.00	(52,115.66)
Temp. Staff	760.86	0.12	0.00	760.86
Rent & Rates & Service	64,918.19	10.43	162,425.00	(97,506.81)
Motor Expenses	225.95	0.04	500.00	(274.05)
Travelling & Entertainment	2,604.70	0.42	6,800.00	(4,195.30)
Print./Stat./Phones/Comp. Supp.	7,259.10	1.17	13,750.00	(6,490.90)

EXAMPLE BUSINESS
Budget Report

Chart of Accounts:

Year to Date

	Actual	Ratio (%)	Budget	Variance
Professional fees	20,842.60	3.35	15,200.00	5,642.60
Equip. Hire & Rental/Comp. Maint.	2,482.66	0.40	2,750.00	(267.34)
Rep. Renewals & Maint.	3,106.60	0.50	2,400.00	706.60
Bank Charges & Interest	18,019.52	2.90	25,700.00	(7,680.48)
Credit Card Charges	2,800.71	0.45	2,875.00	(74.29)
Depreciation	35,420.25	5.69	48,000.00	(12,579.75)
Bad Debts	2,086.50	0.34	0.00	2,086.50
Misc. Subs./Flowers/Clothing/News.	8,202.43	1.32	8,100.00	102.43
Marketing	1,823.82	0.29	6,500.00	(4,676.18)
Training & Seminar Costs	5,782.50	0.93	0.00	5,782.50
Insurance	1,197.00	0.19	0.00	1,197.00
Subsistence	799.95	0.13	0.00	799.95
	281,617.68	45.25	450,400.00	(168,782.32)
Net Profit/(Loss):	141,178.60	22.69	230,750.00	(89,571.40)

Appendix H
Marketing results log

Campaign		Our ref.
Description		
Objectives		
Materials used	Suppliers	

Target and actual results		Target £	Actual £

Activity	Number		
	Income		
	Costs		

X   X   X

Activity Rate		

=   =   =

Activity	Number		
	Income		
	Costs		

X   X   X

Activity Rate		

=   =   =

Activity	Number		
	Income		
	Costs		

Total profit		

Comments and conclusions

Appendix I

Mystery shopper report

Private	Taking NHS	Initial consultation (private)	Routine check-up (private)	Hygienist	Hygiene	Crown	Root canal	Implant in-house	Implant	Ortho. in-house	Ortho.	Rating for Receptionist	Comments	Literature Sent?
Yes	Children	£45 (20-30 mins)	£45 (20-30 mins)	Yes	£55 (25 mins)	from £450 (website)	from £350 (website)	No	from £1,200	No	No	4	Polite enough but little knowledge offered / kept me on hold while she looked up exam prices / no literature offered	No
Yes	Adults & kids	See all NHS 1st time - £16.50 (30 mins)	£45 - 15 mins + £15 per	Yes	£47 (30 mins)	wouldn't quote	wouldn't quote	Yes	£2,200	Yes	£2000 - £2,800	6	Polite and friendly / took address for brochure coming & reg forms / fairly knowledgeable but unwilling to discuss price procedures or prices / told her I was registered as a private patient at present and told they normally register everyone as NHS initially / promoted "lots of in house specialists" including endo, perio, implants, botox. Explained registration process well / said implants are fairly expensive but "highly successful"	No
Yes	No	£35 (45 mins incl xrays)	£40 adult / £15 child (30 mins) + £15 per xray	Yes	£48 (30 mins)	£550 (molar)	£480 (molar)	Yes	from £1,200	Yes	£3000 - £4,000 invisalign	7	Very friendly and polite - impressed with her manner / ready to speak and take time with me when I got through but was on hold for about 1 minute before getting through / has in house ortho on Thurs / promoted invisalign as 'the thing' incl. for kids	Yes

J

Appendix J
Appraisals

> Appraisal form

What motivates you?

Please score out of 10 (1 is low and 10 is high)	Score	What needs to improve in the next 3 months?
How happy are you doing your job?		
Your planning		
Your patient service		
Your technical ability in your role		
Your ability to meet budgets		
Your ability to meet deadlines		
Your ability to cross-sell		
Your relationships with patients		
The type / no. of ideas you generate		
The type / no. of WOWs you generate		
Your ability to follow systems		
Your adaptability to change		
Your passion for the practice vision		

> *Career development review form*

PEOPLE SYSTEMS	Career Development Form
Responsibility of:	**Personnel Manager**
Name:	Date:

Please complete each section below, and return it to ....

by .... If you require more space please add additional lines.

What were your objectives over the last 6 months? How successful were you at meeting these objectives?	My Score 1-10	Reviewer 1-10

What learning have you undertaken in the last 6 months?		
	Learning that has helped me personally	Learning that has helped me at work
Books		
Audio tapes / CDs		
Events / Courses		
Other		

What problems have you encountered meeting your objectives? Have these been solved?

What are your objectives for the next 6 months? (Work)

What are your objectives for the next 6 months? (Life)

What are they for the next 2–3 years?

What can we do to help you achieve these objectives?

Are there any particular areas of training or development you need to undertake to enable you to achieve your objectives?

If you have any other comments, please use this space.

Thank you for completing this form.
PLEASE TAKE A COPY OF THIS FORM FOR YOURSELF AND

SEND/HAND THIS FORM TO ....